everyday

french

cooking

Published in 2001 by
Stewart, Tabori & Chang
A Company of La Martinière Groupe
115 West 18th Street
New York, NY 10011

Library of Congress Cataloging-in-Publication Data
[Cuisine au quotidien. English]
Everyday French cooking / by Christian Constant; introduction by
Linda Dannenberg; illustrations by François Lachèze.
p. cm.
Includes index.
ISBN 1-58479-118-7
1. Cookery, French. I. Title.

TX719.C54 2001
641.5944—dc21
2001042648

The text of this book was composed in Triplex Light.

Printed in Spain.

10 9 8 7 6 5 4 3 2 1

First Printing

Designed by NINA BARNETT

Edited by SANDRA GILBERT
and EMILY VON KOHORN

everyday french cooking

by **CHRISTIAN CONSTANT**

introduction by **LINDA DANNENBERG**

illustrations by **FRANÇOIS LACHÈZE**

stewart, tabori & chang

new york

contents

INTRODUCTION 5

entrées

APPETIZERS 6

LES SOUPES · SOUP 8

LE FOIE GRAS · FOIE GRAS 18

LES LÉGUMES · VEGETABLES 24

LES POISSONS · FISH 32

légumes et pâtes

VEGETABLES AND PASTA 44

coquillages et poissons

SHELLFISH AND FISH 64

volailles et viandes

POULTRY AND MEAT 82

plats uniques

ONE-DISH MEALS 102

desserts

DESSERTS 116

RECIPE INDEX 140

GUIDE TO SPECIALTY STORES 142

CONVERSION CHART 144

INTRODUCTION

by Linda Dannenberg

French cooking is among the most elegant and sophisticated cuisines of the world, and for many it is the food of choice to celebrate life's grand occasions. The traditions and techniques basic to French cooking have influenced and inspired chefs around the world since the eighteenth century. But French cuisine is not just special-occasion fare. For home cooks in France, of course, French cooking is an everyday affair. A cuisine unto itself, French home cooking calls upon the basics of *haute cuisine*—the reverence for fresh products, the classic preparation techniques (often simplified), and the skillful balance of flavors—to enliven even the most unassuming soup, salad, roast chicken, or dessert of fresh berries.

"In France," says Christian Constant, one of France's most celebrated chefs, "there is a real reverence for food, both in a restaurant and at home. People in France spend a great deal of time thinking about food, talking about food, and, finally, in the kitchen preparing food. They also take great care in buying fresh products at local markets and buying the very best they can find. *Faire le marché*—to do the shopping—is one of the most important and fundamental aspects of the cooking process. And quality is key—always think quality!"

Christian Constant is both an apostle for refined, sophisticated contemporary French cuisine, and a lover of simple, unpretentious Gallic home cooking. In the warm, golden ambiance of Le Violon d'Ingres, his plush Paris bistro on the rue Saint-Dominique, just steps from the Eiffel Tower, Constant spins out compelling, delectable dishes such as a Warm Tart of Tiny Baby Vegetables Surrounded by a Frothy Morel Cream Sauce, Delicate Sea Scallops with Truffles, and an Upside-Down Caramelized Pear Tart with a Mille-Feuille Pastry Crust. It is memorable cuisine that earned Constant two coveted Michelin stars just two years after opening his doors in 1997. Previously, Constant was the high-profile chef at Paris' glamorous Hotel Crillon, where he was also awarded two Michelin stars for sublime, classic French cuisine that was, as one critic noted, "perfection at every level." At Le Violon d'Ingres, where perfection still reigns, Constant's cuisine is much more personal, refined, and inventive, informed by the traditions and techniques of classic French cuisine, but fresh and daring. His cuisine is notable for its lightness and balance as well as its elegance and simplicity: elegant products like foie gras are prepared in simple ways, simple products like new potatoes are prepared in elegant ways.

When he's not manning the stove at Le Violon d'Ingres in Paris, Constant revels in the pleasure and simplicity of cooking at home for his wife, Catherine, and young sons Charles and Benjamin, or for Sunday night supper for friends. A native of Montauban, a town in France's deep southwest just north of Toulouse, where the namesake of his Paris restaurant, the painter Ingres, was also born, Constant creates a personal, savory, and inventive cuisine that reflects a distinctive southwestern influence. It is this homey fare that *Everyday French Cooking* celebrates with dishes such as Cream of Lentil Soup Garnished with Bacon, Croutons, and Chives; Roast Turkey with Truffle, Chestnut, and Chipolata Sausage Stuffing; Nut-Crusted Baked Salmon with Lamb's Lettuce Salad; Broccoli and Cauliflower Gratin with Ham; and Sautéed Cherries with Vanilla Ice Cream.

Constant focuses on his personalized French home cooking featuring great recipes for everyday, with many inventive dishes that are easy and quick to prepare. Christian Constant's *Everyday French Cooking* gives a new perspective to contemporary French cuisine, with captivating recipes that will please the palate and brighten the home table, whether the occasion is a simple Sunday supper or a festive anniversary brunch, a weekend lunch for two or a birthday bash for ten.

entrées

APPETIZERS

LES SOUPES • SOUP

LE FOIE GRAS • FOIE GRAS

LES LÉGUMES • VEGETABLES

LES POISSONS • FISH

pureed vegetable and herb soup

SERVES 6

For the soup base:
3 carrots, peeled and finely
  diced
2 zucchini, peeled and finely
  diced
1/3 pound white button mushrooms, finely
  chopped
2 stalks celery, finely diced
3 medium onions, finely diced
2 turnips, peeled and finely diced
1/4 head green cabbage, finely chopped
1 pound ripe tomatoes, peeled, seeded, and
  chopped
2 medium leeks, white and pale green parts
  only, thoroughly rinsed to remove grit,
  finely chopped

1 bulb fennel, outer layers removed, finely
  chopped
Coarse salt
Freshly ground black pepper
5 cardamom seeds
1 3/4 cups half-and-half
Fine sea salt

For the herb puree:
Coarse salt
2 bunches chervil, leaves and tiny stems only
3 bunches dill, leaves and tiny stems only
2 bunches tarragon, leaves and tiny stems
  only
2 bunches flat-leaf parsley, leaves and tiny
  stems only

PREPARE THE SOUP BASE: In a large soup pot or casserole, combine the carrots, zucchini, mushrooms, celery, onions, turnips, cabbage, tomatoes, leeks, and fennel with 4 quarts cold water. Add a generous pinch of coarse salt, several turns of the pepper mill, and the cardamom. Bring to a boil over high heat, then reduce the heat to medium-low and cook at a very gentle boil for 45 minutes. Remove from the heat, then press through a food mill or a very fine strainer into a large pot. Add the half-and-half and stir well to incorporate. Bring to a boil over medium-high heat, reduce the heat to medium-low, and simmer for 10 to 15 minutes. Adjust the seasoning with the fine salt and pepper to taste; set aside.

MEANWHILE, PREPARE THE HERB PUREE: Fill a medium pot with cold water, add a generous pinch of coarse salt, and bring the water to a boil over high heat. Add the chervil, dill, tarragon, and parsley and cook for 5 minutes. Remove from the heat, immediately add cold water to the pot to stop the cooking, then drain. Transfer the herbs to the bowl of a small food processor, and process for 8 to 10 seconds, until the mixture forms a smooth puree.

Add the puree to the vegetable soup and stir well to incorporate. Raise the heat under the soup pot, and heat, stirring constantly, until very hot but not boiling. Transfer to a warmed soup tureen or ladle into warmed individual soup plates, and serve immediately.

hearty tomato soup with vermicelli and olive oil garnish

SERVES 4 TO 6

3 medium Idaho potatoes, peeled and coarsely chopped
1 large onion, coarsely chopped
6 large red-ripe tomatoes, coarsely chopped
Fine sea salt
Freshly ground black pepper
$^1/_4$ cup broken-up vermicelli
2 tablespoons extra-virgin olive oil

In a large pot, combine the potatoes, onion, and tomatoes with 6$^1/_2$ cups cold water. Add a generous pinch of salt and several turns of the pepper mill, bring to a boil over high heat, then reduce the heat to medium-low and simmer for 35 minutes.

Remove from the heat and transfer the mixture, working in two or three batches, to the bowl of a food mill or a fine strainer set over a clean pot. Press the mixture into the pot, then bring the mixture to a boil over medium-high heat. Add the vermicelli, reduce the heat to medium, and cook for 10 minutes. Adjust the seasoning to taste, then transfer the soup to a warmed soup tureen; drizzle the oil over the top but do *not* mix in. Serve immediately.

CHEF'S SUGGESTION: If you cannot find perfectly ripe tomatoes, pick the best available, and add 1 teaspoon tomato concentrate just after you bring the vegetables to a boil, stirring to incorporate.

chestnut soup with foie gras, cabbage, white beans, and porcini mushrooms

SERVES 6

1/2 cup dried Great Northern or navy beans, soaked overnight in water, drained
1/2 medium onion intact, plus 1 medium onion, finely chopped
2 carrots, peeled and cut into quarters
1 clove garlic, peeled
1 bouquet garni (1 sprig thyme, 1 bay leaf, 1 sprig parsley, 1 small leek, pale green
and white parts only), tied in cheesecloth
1/2 pound canned chestnuts, drained
4 tablespoons unsalted butter
1 stalk celery
Fine sea salt
1 tablespoon goose fat, or 2 teaspoons unsalted butter with 1 teaspoon olive oil
1/2 pound fresh porcini mushrooms or cremini mushrooms, cleaned, stems trimmed, chopped
3 leaves green cabbage, sliced into fine julienne
4 1/4 cups chicken stock
1 tablespoon finely chopped parsley
Six 2-ounce slices raw foie gras duck liver
Freshly ground black pepper

In a medium saucepan, combine the beans with the half onion, the carrots, garlic, and bouquet garni. Cover with cold water, bring to a boil over high heat, then reduce the heat to medium-low, cover, and cook, stirring occasionally. After 1 1/2 hours, drain the beans, discarding the onion, garlic, and the bouquet garni; remove the carrots and set aside; set the beans aside.

Meanwhile, in a medium saucepan, combine the chestnuts with the butter, celery, and a pinch of salt, cover with cold water, and bring to a boil over high heat. Reduce the heat to medium-low and cook for 30 minutes; drain, discard the celery, and set aside.

In a large skillet, heat the goose fat over medium heat. Add the mushrooms and the chopped onion and cook, stirring constantly, until the mushrooms soften slightly and the onions begin to turn translucent, about 4 minutes. Finely dice the reserved carrots and add them to the skillet, then add the cabbage and 1½ cups of the stock and stir to combine. Cook, stirring frequently, until the liquid is completely evaporated. Sprinkle on the parsley, stir to combine, then remove from the heat and set aside.

In a medium skillet, heat the remaining stock to boiling over medium-high heat. Reduce the heat to medium, gently place the slices of foie gras in the stock, and cook for exactly 2 minutes; remove the pan from the heat. Divide the beans and the vegetable mixture among 6 warmed soup bowls. Place a foie gras slice in the center of each bowl. Return the stock to a boil, transfer to the bowl of a food processor or blender, add the chestnuts, and puree until smooth. Ladle over the foie gras and vegetables, season with salt and pepper to taste, and serve immediately.

chilled cream of lima bean soup with rosemary

SERVES 6

2 pounds fresh baby lima beans, shelled; or 1 pound frozen baby lima beans
1 carrot, peeled and sliced into 1-inch rounds
3 cloves garlic, peeled
$^{1}/_{3}$ pound lean slab bacon, in one piece
1 bouquet garni (1 sprig thyme, 1 bay leaf, 1 sprig parsley, 1 small leek, white and pale green parts only), tied in cheesecloth
1 whole clove
1 medium onion
5 cups chicken stock
2 cups heavy cream
Fine sea salt
Freshly ground black pepper
2 tablespoons unsalted butter
2 slices dense white sandwich bread, crusts trimmed, cut into $^{1}/_{4}$-inch cubes
3 tablespoons chopped chives
1 sprig rosemary, leaves only, minced
1$^{1}/_{2}$ ounces black truffles, chopped (optional)

In a stockpot, combine the lima beans, carrot, garlic, bacon, and bouquet garni. Press the clove into one end of the onion and add to the pot, then pour in the stock and the cream. Bring the mixture to a simmer over medium heat, then reduce the heat to medium-low, cover, and simmer for 1$^{1}/_{2}$ hours, stirring occasionally and skimming the top frequently.

Remove the pot from the heat, then remove the bacon and reserve for another use or discard. Pour the remaining mixture into a large strainer or a colander lined with cheesecloth set over a large bowl, and press through gently with the back of a ladle. Season the liquid with salt and pepper. Cover the bowl with plastic wrap and refrigerate for at least 2 hours, until ready to serve.

Meanwhile, make the croutons: In a medium skillet, melt the butter over medium heat, then add the bread cubes, stir to coat with the butter, and sauté until golden brown. Transfer to a plate and set aside.

To serve, transfer the soup to a tureen. Divide the croutons, chives, rosemary, and truffles, if using, among 6 soup bowls, placing the garnish in the center of the bowls. At the table, ladle the soup over the garnish and serve immediately.

CHEF'S SUGGESTION: Light and delicate, this is an appealing summertime soup, perfect to serve when garden-fresh beans are available.

cream of pumpkin soup with diced gruyère and buttered croutons

SERVES 4

³/4 cup unsalted butter, cut into 12 tablespoons
1 medium onion, minced
2 pounds fresh pumpkin, peeled, seeded,
   coarsely chopped
3 cups chicken stock
2 cups half-and-half
Fine sea salt
Freshly ground black pepper
¹/4 cup unsalted butter, melted and clarified
2 slices dense white sandwich bread crusts removed,
   cut into ¹/4-inch cubes
¹/3 pound Gruyère cheese, cut into ¹/4-inch cubes
1 bunch chives, finely chopped
1 sprig rosemary, leaves only, minced

In a small, heavy-bottomed soup pot or casserole, melt 2 tablespoons of butter over medium heat. Add the onion and cook, stirring frequently, until softened and slightly translucent but not browned, about 4 minutes. Add the pumpkin, stock, and half-and-half and stir to combine. Season generously with salt and pepper, reduce heat to medium-low, and cook 30 minutes, stirring occasionally. Remove from the heat, then transfer the mixture to the bowl of a food processor. Puree 10 to 12 seconds, until the mixture is very smooth. Pour through a fine strainer or chinois into a clean pot. Add 6 tablespoons of the butter and stir to combine; the butter will slowly melt into the soup. Keep warm over low heat.

In a small skillet, warm the remaining 4 tablespoons butter over medium heat until gently bubbling. Add the bread cubes, stir to coat with the butter and sauté until golden brown. Using a slotted spoon or spatula, transfer croutons to a small bowl.

Raise the heat under the soup to medium-high, and heat for several minutes until very hot but not boiling, stirring frequently with a whisk to blend the butter and keep the soup from burning on the bottom of the pot. Transfer to a warmed soup tureen. Sprinkle on the diced Gruyère, croutons, chives and rosemary; or ladle into individual soup bowls, garnishing as in the tureen. Serve immediately.

CHEF'S SUGGESTION: To save a little time and effort, replace the fresh pumpkin with one 16-ounce can of pumpkin puree, and reduce the cooking time from 30 to 15 minutes.

essence of langoustine soup

SERVES 6

3 tablespoons extra-virgin olive oil
2 pounds langoustine, prawn, or crayfish heads (have your fishmonger save some
for you if you don't have some in reserve), lightly crushed
1 onion, minced
1 shallot, minced
2 tomatoes, chopped
$^{1}/_{4}$ pound parsley sprigs
1 teaspoon tomato paste
2 cups chicken stock
$^{1}/_{4}$ cup cognac (optional)
4 tablespoons unsalted butter, cut into bits
$^{1}/_{2}$ cup crème fraîche, whipped to soft peaks
Fine sea salt
Freshly ground black pepper

In a large skillet, heat the oil over medium heat. Add the langoustine heads, onion, shallot, tomatoes, and parsley and stir to combine. Sauté, stirring constantly, until the onion and shallot begin to turn translucent, but not brown, about 4 minutes. Add the tomato concentrate and stock, stir to incorporate, and cook at a simmer for 20 minutes. Add the cognac, if using, increase the heat to high and bring soup to the boiling point, then remove from the heat and pour the mixture through a fine strainer into a large, warmed mixing bowl, pressing gently on the solids with the back of a ladle. Add the butter and crème fraîche and stir gently just to combine. Season to taste with salt and pepper. Using a hand-held mixer, beat the soup until a foamy mousse forms on top. Ladle into warmed soup bowls and serve immediately.

CHEF'S SUGGESTION: This recipe puts to good use langoustine or prawn heads—full of flavor—that are generally discarded. You can enhance the flavor of the soup, giving it more depth and sophistication, by adding $^{1}/_{4}$ cup cognac at the end of the cooking time. For an unusual hors d'oeuvre, serve small portions of soup in teacups with saucers; the foam on top makes it look like a cappuccino.

salt cod, leek, and potato soup with chorizo garnish

Begin soaking the salt cod a day before serving.

1 tablespoon olive oil
$^{1}/_{2}$ pound leeks, trimmed, white and pale green parts only, well washed
to remove grit, and finely chopped
$^{1}/_{2}$ pound Idaho potatoes, peeled and finely chopped
$^{1}/_{4}$ pound salt cod, soaked in cold water for 24 hours to de-salt,
drained, patted dry, and coarsely chopped
4 cups chicken stock
1 cup light cream
Fine sea salt
Freshly ground black pepper
1 clove garlic, halved
18 ($^{1}/_{4}$-inch) slices baguette bread, toasted
$^{1}/_{4}$ pound chorizo sausage, cooked and very finely chopped

In a heavy-bottom casserole or small stock pot, warm the oil over medium heat, then add the leeks and potatoes and stir to combine. Sauté, stirring constantly, for 3 minutes, then add the cod and stir to combine. Add the stock, stir, then cook for 20 minutes, stirring occasionally. Add the cream, reduce the heat to low, and simmer for 10 minutes. Remove from the heat and transfer the mixture to a food mill set over a clean pot, and press through. (If you don't have a food mill, puree in a food processor until just smooth.) Season to taste with salt and pepper, then bring to a boil over medium-high heat.

Meanwhile, gently rub the garlic clove over one side of the baguette slices and arrange in a bread basket. Ladle the soup into warmed serving bowls, sprinkle the chorizo on top, and serve immediately, accompanied by the garlic-scented baguette slices.

cream of lentil soup garnished with bacon, croutons, and chives

½ pound (about 1 cup) imported French green lentils, picked over and well rinsed
1 carrot, peeled and sliced into 1-inch rounds
6 whole cloves garlic, peeled
⅓ pound lean bacon, in one piece
1 bouquet garni (1 sprig thyme, 1 bay leaf, 1 sprig parsley, 1 small leek, white and pale green parts only), tied in a double layer of cheesecloth
1 whole clove

1 medium onion
8 cups chicken stock
2 tablespoons unsalted butter
2 slices dense white sandwich bread, crusts trimmed, cut into ¼-inch dice
1 cup crème fraîche plus 1½ cups light cream, blended; or 2½ cups heavy cream
Fine sea salt
Freshly ground black pepper
3 tablespoons chopped chives

In a soup pot, combine the lentils, carrot, garlic, bacon, and bouquet garni. Press the clove into one end of the onion and add to the pot, then fill with cold water to cover. Bring to a boil over high heat, then drain the water and add the stock. Bring the stock to a boil over medium-high heat, then reduce the heat to medium-low, cover, and simmer for 30 minutes.

Meanwhile, make the croutons: In a medium skillet, melt the butter over medium heat, then add the bread, stir to coat with the butter, and sauté until golden brown. Transfer to a plate and set aside.

Remove the soup pot from the heat, then remove the bacon and set aside; remove and discard the onion, carrot, and bouquet garni, leaving just the garlic in the pot with the lentils. Add the crème fraîche mixture, stir to combine, then add salt and pepper to taste. Bring to a simmer over medium heat, and cook for 10 minutes. Meanwhile, very finely dice the bacon, place in a small skillet over medium heat, and brown until crisp; drain on a double layer of paper towels and set aside.

Remove the soup from the heat and pass it through a food mill into a bowl; or puree it in a food processor until smooth. Pour the mixture through a fine strainer into a large, clean saucepan and bring to a simmer over medium-high heat. Transfer the soup to a warmed tureen or ladle into warmed soup dishes, and sprinkle the bacon, croutons, and chives over the top. Serve immediately.

CHEF'S SUGGESTION: This soup is tasty served either warm or cold. Try it chilled on a warm summer evening.

terrine of duck foie gras

SERVES 4

¾ pound raw foie gras duck liver
2 tablespoons cognac
1½ teaspoons fine sea salt
Freshly ground assorted (pink, green, black) or black pepper

CLEAN THE DUCK LIVER: With a small, sharp knife, cut away and discard the liver's thin, transparent skin. Gently pull out and discard the large artery and attached capillaries.

In a plastic storage container or a covered ceramic terrine, combine the liver, cognac, salt, and 3 turns of the pepper mill. Cover and refrigerate for 12 hours.

Preheat the oven to 300° F. Fill a deep roasting pan with water halfway up the sides. If the foie gras is not in a ceramic terrine, transfer to one with any liquid. Place the terrine in the center of the roasting pan, add water to come three-quarters up the sides of the terrine, and place the pan in the center of the oven. Cook for 40 minutes, then test for doneness: slide the tip of a small butter knife into the center of the foie gras and bring it to your lips; the blade should feel warm but not hot. If the blade is not quite warm, return the foie gras to the oven for another 5 minutes and test again. Remove the terrine to a wire rack to cool. Refrigerate overnight; serve within 48 hours.

CHEF'S SUGGESTION: Serve accompanied by thin, toasted slices of country bread.

carpaccio of marinated duck foie gras

SERVES 6

Begin preparations for this recipe one day before serving.

1 pound raw foie gras duck liver
$^1/_2$ pound coarse sea salt
4 tablespoons black peppercorns, crushed
1 sprig thyme
1 bay leaf
1 clove garlic, quartered
Freshly ground black pepper
1 tablespoon sherry wine vinegar
Fleur de sel or fine sea salt
3 tablespoons extra-virgin olive oil

Clean the duck liver as described on page 18. On a large plate, combine the coarse sea salt and crushed peppercorns. Place the liver on the plate and press into the salt and pepper. Turn the liver and press on the other side. Repeat until all parts of the liver are coated. Place the thyme, bay leaf, and garlic on top of the liver. Cover the plate with plastic wrap and refrigerate for 24 hours.

Rinse the liver well under cold running water until all the salt and pepper are removed. Dry carefully with a cotton towel. Season generously with several turns of the pepper mill, cover lightly with plastic wrap, and refrigerate for 3 or 4 hours.

Just before serving, cut the duck liver into very thin slices, using a very sharp knife to cut cleanly through the liver. Divide among 6 serving plates. Make a sherry vinaigrette by combining the vinegar in a small bowl with a generous pinch of fleur de sel, and whisk to combine. Add the oil and whisk to emulsify. Drizzle the vinaigrette equally over the 6 portions of marinated foie gras and serve immediately.

CHEF'S SUGGESTION: You can accompany the carpaccio of foie gras with a simple, elegant green salad, such as lamb's lettuce tossed with sherry vinaigrette. Or serve it as an hors d'oeuvre, atop small slices of toasted country bread, to accompany *aperitifs*.

warm fresh duck foie gras with caramelized grapes

Six 3- to 4-ounce slices raw foie gras duck liver
Fine sea salt
Freshly ground black pepper
1 small bunch (about 1 pound) seedless green grapes
2 tablespoons confectioners' sugar
$3/4$ cup Muscat white wine or other sweet white wine
1 cup duck stock or chicken stock

Preheat the oven to 425° F. Clean the liver as described on page 18. Season the liver slices with salt and pepper. Place them in a heavy-bottom flameproof enameled baking dish or casserole and bake in the center of the oven for 3 minutes; turn the slices and bake for another 3 minutes. Transfer the slices to a plate covered with paper towels; remove most of the accumulated fat and reserve for another use, leaving about 1 tablespoon fat in the pan.

Place the pan over medium heat, add the grapes, and stir to coat, then sprinkle with the confectioners' sugar. Cook, stirring frequently, until the grapes are lightly caramelized, about 4 minutes. Add the wine and the stock, stir to combine, and cook, stirring frequently, until the sauce reduces slightly and starts to thicken, about 6 minutes. Meanwhile, arrange the foie gras slices on 6 warmed serving plates. Adjust the seasoning of the sauce, then spoon over the foie gras slices, dividing the grapes equally among the portions, and serve immediately.

confit of duck foie gras

Begin preparations for this recipe at least two days before serving.

1¹/3 pounds raw foie gras duck liver
3 ounces (about ¹/2 cup) fleur de sel or coarse sea salt, plus additional
Coarsely ground black pepper
2 whole cloves
1 clove garlic
1 teaspoon whole black peppercorns
4 cups duck fat, at room temperature (see Guide to Specialty Stores, page 142)
1 tablespoon sherry wine vinegar
3 tablespoons extra-virgin olive oil
¹/4 pound mixed baby greens or mesclun salad greens
2 ounces shelled walnuts, halved
¹/2 bunch chervil, leaves only

Clean the liver as described on page 18. Coat all sides of the liver with 3 ounces of fleur de sel and a generous amount of coarsely ground black pepper. Place in a ceramic dish, cover with plastic wrap, and refrigerate for 24 hours.

Preheat the oven to 150° F or the lowest oven setting. Using a cotton towel, carefully wipe the liver to remove most of the salt and pepper. Place the liver in a heavy-bottom enameled pot just large enough to hold the liver and the duck fat. Add the cloves, garlic, and peppercorns. Top with the duck fat, smoothing it over to cover the liver completely. Place the pot over low heat; the temperature of the duck fat should rise to just 150° F; use an instant-read thermometer to check. Cook for 1¹/2 hours, carefully maintaining the temperature of the fat at 150° F during the entire cooking time. (The succulent texture of the foie gras will be destroyed at a higher temperature.) Transfer the pot to a wire rack to cool. Cover with plastic wrap and refrigerate for at least 1 day.

Just before serving, gently wipe off the foie gras. Sprinkle lightly with a pinch of fleur de sel and several turns of the pepper mill. Cut the foie gras into 12 thin slices. In a small bowl combine a pinch of fleur de sel and the vinegar and whisk to combine. Add the oil and whisk to emulsify. Pour over the greens and toss well. Divide the salad among 6 serving plates. Arrange 2 foie gras slices atop the salad on each plate. Garnish with the walnuts and chervil leaves and serve immediately.

CHEF'S SUGGESTION: While you can serve the foie gras after just a day in the refrigerator, it is even more flavorful if you leave it there for several days, or up to a week, before serving.

sautéed duck foie gras with gingerbread coating

SERVES 6

2/3 pound mixed field greens
2 shallots, thinly sliced
1/4 bunch chervil, leaves only, chopped
1/4 bunch chives, chopped
1/4 bunch tarragon, leaves only, chopped
8 tablespoons sherry wine vinegar
Fine sea salt
Freshly ground black pepper
5 tablespoons olive oil
Six 2-ounce slices raw duck foie gras, blotted dry
2 egg yolks, beaten
2 cups finely crumbled gingerbread
2 cups veal demi-glace (see Guide to Specialty Stores, page 142), or 4 cups
beef stock cooked to reduce by half
1 crisp Macoun, Cortland, or McIntosh apple, peeled, cored, and julienned
2 cooked beets, peeled and julienned
2 tablespoons unsalted butter

In a salad bowl, combine the field greens, shallots, chervil, chives, and tarragon. In a small bowl, combine 2 tablespoons of the vinegar and generous pinches of salt and pepper and whisk to dissolve the salt. Add the oil and whisk to emulsify. Set aside.

Preheat the oven to 400° F. Season the foie gras slices with salt and pepper and place in a shallow, ovenproof baking dish. Place in the center of the oven and bake for 4 minutes, turn the slices over and bake for another 4 minutes. Remove from the oven, brush the foie gras slices with the egg yolk on both sides and dredge in the gingerbread crumbs. Transfer the slices to a clean plate and set aside.

Place the baking dish over medium-high heat on top of the stove, pour in the remaining 6 tablespoons vinegar, and deglaze, scraping up the browned bits stuck to the dish. Add the demi-glace and cook for 5 to 6 minutes, stirring. Taste to adjust the seasonings, then pour through a fine-mesh sieve into a warmed bowl.

Toss the mixed greens with the vinaigrette. Divide the salad among 4 plates. Sprinkle the julienned apple and beet on top.

In a heavy skillet, melt the butter over medium-high heat. Add the crumb-coated foie gras and cook for 1 minute on each side. Place a slice of foie gras alongside the salad on each plate, spoon the reserved sauce around it, and serve.

provençal tomato tart
with tapenade

SERVES 6

2 pounds firm, ripe plum tomatoes, seeded and quartered lengthwise
6 tablespoons extra-virgin olive oil
2 teaspoons thyme leaves
2 cloves garlic, finely chopped
2 bay leaves
Fine sea salt
Freshly ground black pepper
7 anchovy fillets, drained
4 ounces (about 2/3 cup) oil-cured black olives, pitted
4 onions, finely chopped
2 teaspoons sherry vinegar
10 ounces prepared puff pastry dough
2 ounces Parmesan cheese, grated into large shavings

Preheat the oven to 175° F, or the lowest setting. Arrange the tomatoes on a greased baking sheet, drizzle with 3 tablespoons of the oil, scatter the thyme and half the garlic over the tomatoes, add the bay leaves and season with salt and pepper. Bake in the center of the oven for 2 hours. Set aside on a wire rack to cool; discard the thyme and bay leaves.

Meanwhile, prepare the tapenade: in the bowl of a small food processor, combine the remaining garlic, 1 anchovy fillet, the olives, and 1 tablespoon of the oil. Process, adding 2 more tablespoons of the oil in a thin stream as you process, until the mixture is coarsely pureed. Set aside.

In a medium skillet, heat 2 tablespoons of the oil over medium heat. Add the onions, reduce the heat to medium-low, and sauté, stirring frequently, until they are softened and slightly colored, 5 to 7 minutes. Add the vinegar and deglaze the pan, stirring to combine well with the onions, then remove from the heat and set aside. (The recipe can be prepared several hours in advance up to this point.)

Preheat the oven to 350° F. On a lightly floured work surface, using a floured rolling pin, roll out the puff pastry dough into a rough circle about $^1/_8$ inch thick and about 12 inches in diameter. Place the pastry dough on a very lightly greased baking sheet. Place another baking sheet directly on top of the pastry dough and bake in the center of the oven for 10 minutes. Transfer to a wire rack to cool slightly. Using a dinner plate, lid, or tart pan as your guide, trim the puff pastry into a 10-inch circle; set aside.

Just before serving, preheat the oven to 350° F. Spread the onion mixture evenly over the top of the pastry circle. On top of the onion mixture, arrange the tomato pieces in overlapping concentric circles, working from the outside in. Arrange the remaining 6 anchovy fillets like the spokes of a wheel on top of the tomatoes, then sprinkle on the Parmesan shavings. Bake just long enough for the Parmesan to soften, 3 to 5 minutes. Serve immediately, accompanied by the tapenade.

celery root in parsley-mustard mayonnaise

SERVES 6

1 egg yolk, at room temperature
1 tablespoon Dijon mustard, at room temperature
1 tablespoon white-wine vinegar
Fine sea salt
Freshly ground black pepper
1 cup peanut oil
1 tablespoon minced parsley
1 small celery root, about 1 pound, peeled, coarsely grated in a food processor or
with a Mouli grater, and tossed with juice of $^1/_2$ lemon to prevent oxidation

PREPARE THE MAYONNAISE: In a mixing bowl, combine the egg yolk, mustard, vinegar, a pinch of salt, and several turns of the pepper mill. Beat with a whisk until slightly thickened and smoothly blended. Add a few drops of the oil and whisk to blend; add a few more drops and whisk until blended and thickened. Add the remaining oil very slowly, in slow, steady stream, beating until the mixture emulsifies. Add the parsley and stir in with a wooden spoon. The recipe can be made several hours ahead up to this point and refrigerated, covered with plastic wrap, until ready to use.

Place the celery root in a salad bowl, add the mayonnaise, and toss to coat well. Adjust the seasoning to taste and serve immediately, or cover with plastic wrap and refrigerate until ready to serve.

CHEF'S SUGGESTION: This recipe makes a mayonnaise using raw egg. If you prefer not to use raw egg, and also to simplify the recipe, you can substitute 1 cup good-quality commercial mayonnaise such as Hellmann's for the mayonnaise preparation, stirring in 1 tablespoon finely minced parsley and 1 tablespoon Dijon mustard before combining it with the grated celery root.

sautéed hearts of baby artichokes

SERVES 4

Juice of $^1/_2$ lemon
16 baby artichokes
5 tablespoons extra-virgin olive oil
2 cloves garlic, minced
1 shallot, finely chopped
1 teaspoon coriander seeds
$^1/_2$ cup white wine
$^3/_4$ cup chicken stock
4 teaspoons balsamic vinegar
Fine sea salt
Freshly ground black pepper
4 teaspoons chopped herb mixture: chervil, chives, flat-leaf parsley

Fill a large bowl with cold water, and stir in the lemon juice. Trim the leaves, choke, and all but $^1/_2$ inch of the stem from the artichokes and place them in the bowl of water as you work. Drain the artichokes, pat them dry, then cut into quarters. In a large skillet, heat 3 tablespoons of the oil over medium heat. Add the artichokes and sauté, stirring frequently, for 5 minutes. Add the garlic, shallot, and coriander seeds and stir to combine. Pour in the wine and stock and stir, scraping up any browned bits stuck to the pan. Simmer for 5 minutes, stirring occasionally, then remove from the heat.

Divide the artichokes and the broth among 4 warmed soup plates. Drizzle the balsamic vinegar and remaining 2 tablespoons oil over the artichokes, season generously with salt and pepper, sprinkle the chopped herbs over, and serve.

CHEF'S SUGGESTION: To save time, or if fresh baby artichokes are not available, you can substitute frozen baby artichokes; thaw before using.

artichoke bottoms with celery root puree and marrow

SERVES 6

6 large artichokes
Juice of $^1/_2$ lemon
3 tablespoons olive oil, plus additional
3 tablespoons unsalted butter, softened
1 medium celery root, peeled and cut into fine dice
1 onion, minced
4 cups chicken stock
2 tablespoons crème fraîche
Salt
Freshly ground black pepper
1 cup white wine
$4^1/_2$ ounces thick-sliced bacon, cut in a large dice
1 slice dense white bread, cut into small cubes
6 slices beef marrow, about $^1/_2$ inch thick (available from a butcher)
Fleur de sel or coarse sea salt
6 tablespoons double-strength rich chicken stock, heated

Remove and discard the artichoke leaves. Using a sharp paring knife, trim away the choke. Trim the edges of the hearts, then keep them in cool water mixed with the lemon juice.

In a saucepan, heat 2 tablespoons of the oil and 1 tablespoon of the butter over medium heat. Add the celery root and onion, stir to coat, then pour in 2 cups of the stock and cook for about 30 minutes, or until the celery root is tender. Pass the mixture through a food mill or puree in a food processor. Transfer the mixture to a bowl and stir in the crème fraîche and 1 tablespoon of the butter. Season to taste with salt and pepper and keep warm.

Put the artichoke hearts in a heavy casserole with the remaining 1 tablespoon oil and cook over medium-high heat until browned. Add the wine and cook until the liquid evaporates. Add the remaining 2 cups stock, season with salt and pepper, and cook for 30 minutes, or until the artichokes are tender. Keep warm.

In a small skillet, cook the bacon until crisp, then drain on paper towels. Wipe out the skillet, melt the remaining 1 tablespoon butter, stir in the bread cubes, and sauté until golden brown.

In a medium skillet, bring some water to a simmer. Add the marrow and simmer for 2 to 3 minutes. Place a warm artichoke bottom on each of 6 plates and spoon the hot celery root puree into them. Place a slice of marrow on top. Season with fleur de sel and pepper. Sprinkle on the croutons and bacon. Spoon a tablespoon of reduced stock and a thin ribbon of olive oil around each artichoke heart and serve.

vegetable tempura with soy-flavored tartar sauce

SERVES 8

For the tartar sauce:
1 tablespoon capers, drained and finely chopped
1 tablespoon cornichons, drained and finely chopped
2 hard-cooked eggs, finely chopped
1 tablespoon minced parsley
1 cup mayonnaise
2 tablespoons soy sauce

For the tempura:
2^1/2 cups self-rising cake flour
1 green bell pepper, cut into ^{1}/2-by-2^1/2-inch pieces
1 red bell pepper, cut into ^{1}/2-by-2^1/2-inch pieces
1 firm eggplant, peeled and cut into ^{1}/2-by-^{1}/2-by-2^1/2-inch pieces
1 large zucchini, cut into ^{1}/2-by-^{1}/2-by-2^1/2-inch pieces
Fine sea salt
Freshly ground black pepper
1 basil leaf
2 quarts olive oil

PREPARE THE TARTAR SAUCE: Put the capers, cornichons, and eggs in a mixing bowl and combine. Add the parsley, mayonnaise, and soy sauce and stir until well blended. Set aside.

PREPARE THE TEMPURA: Fill a mixing bowl with 2^1/3 cups plus 1 tablespoon ice water. Sift the cake flour over the water and stir gently until the batter is smooth. Refrigerate the batter for 30 minutes.

Season the vegetables with salt and pepper. Heat the oil in a deep-fat fryer or wok. Dip each vegetable piece in the batter, letting any excess batter run off, then transfer them to the deep-fat fryer basket and lower them into the hot oil; if using a wok, place vegetables directly into the oil. Do the same with the basil. When the vegetables are golden brown, remove the basket, if using, or remove vegetables with a slotted spoon, and drain the pieces on paper towels. Work in batches if necessary. Season with salt and pepper and serve immediately with the tartar sauce.

asparagus fricassee with soft-boiled egg

SERVES 6

3 tablespoons unsalted butter
3 slices dense white sandwich bread, cut into $^1/_2$-inch cubes
6 eggs
$^1/_2$ pound beef marrow, chilled, finely diced
$^1/_3$ pound slab bacon, cut into pieces 1 inch long and $^1/_4$ inch thick
$^3/_4$ cup double-strength chicken stock (reduce 1$^1/_2$ cups regular chicken stock by half)
2 pounds thin asparagus, trimmed and cut on the diagonal into 1-inch lengths
Fleur de sel or coarse sea salt

In a medium skillet, melt 2 tablespoons of the butter over medium heat. Add the bread and sauté, stirring frequently, until the bread is crisp and golden brown, about 5 minutes. Remove from the heat and set aside.

Bring a medium saucepan of water to a boil over high heat. Using a tablespoon, gently place the eggs in the pan. Reduce the heat to medium-high and boil the eggs for 5 minutes. Drain and immediately refresh the eggs with cold water and set aside in the pan.

In a large skillet, melt the remaining 1 tablespoon butter over medium heat. Add the marrow and bacon and cook, stirring frequently, until the bacon is golden brown on all sides, about 5 minutes. Add the stock and deglaze the pan, scraping up any browned bits stuck to the pan. Cook until the mixture begins to simmer, then add the asparagus and cook until the asparagus is tender, about 4 minutes. Meanwhile, peel the eggs.

Divide the asparagus mixture among 6 warmed soup plates. Place a boiled egg in the center of each plate and puncture with a fork just enough so that yolk begins to flow out. Sprinkle each serving with a pinch of fleur de sel, scatter the croutons on top, and serve immediately.

lemon-marinated fresh anchovies

SERVES 4

Juice of 3 lemons
Fleur de sel or fine sea salt
Freshly ground black pepper
1¹/3 pounds fresh anchovy fillets, meticulously boned
2 baby onions, or 1 small Vidalia onion, minced
1 teaspoon minced garlic
1 small, mild red chili pepper or small sweet red pepper, minced
1 tablespoon minced flat-leaf parsley

Pour half the lemon juice over the surface of a large plate. Sprinkle a generous pinch of fleur de sel and 3 or 4 turns of the pepper mill over the lemon juice. Lay the anchovy fillets in a single layer over the lemon juice. Sprinkle the onions, garlic, red pepper, and parsley evenly over the fillets. Drizzle on the remaining lemon juice. Season with fleur de sel and pepper, cover lightly with plastic wrap, and refrigerate for at least 30 minutes, and up to about 2 hours. Divide the fillets among 4 serving plates, drizzle with some of the marinade, and serve.

mussels en papillote

SERVES 6

2 1/2 pounds mussels, washed and scrubbed in cold water
3 shallots, finely chopped
2 cloves garlic, minced
1 tablespoon minced parsley
2 sprigs fresh thyme
1 small bay leaf
1/2 cup dry white wine
2 tablespoons olive oil
1 tablespoon unsalted butter
Juice of 1/2 lemon
Freshly ground black pepper

Preheat the oven to 400° F. Place the mussels in the center of a large (26-by-18-inch) sheet of heavy-duty aluminum foil, and fold the edges up to make vertical side walls. Sprinkle on the shallots, garlic, and parsley. Add the thyme, bay leaf, wine, oil, butter, lemon juice, and several turns of the pepper mill. Seal the foil packet: bring the 2 shorter edges of the foil together above the mussels and fold them over on themselves 3 times, being careful not to squeeze the mussels together; they need plenty of room inside to open. Seal the 2 sides securely. Place in the center of the oven and cook for 8 minutes. Transfer the foil packet to a large warmed ceramic serving bowl and bring to the table. Open the foil packet and serve immediately, dividing the mussels and broth among 6 warmed soup plates; discard any unopened mussels and the bay leaf.

clams with thyme en papillote

1^3/4 pounds clams, washed and scrubbed in cold water
3 shallots, finely chopped
2 cloves garlic, minced
1 tablespoon minced parsley
2 sprigs fresh thyme
1 small bay leaf
^{1}/2 cup dry white wine
2 tablespoons olive oil
1 tablespoon unsalted butter
Juice of ^{1}/2 lemon
Freshly ground black pepper

Preheat the oven to 400° F. Place the clams in the center of a large (26-by-18-inch) sheet of heavy-duty aluminum foil, and fold the edges up to make vertical side walls. Sprinkle on the shallots, garlic, and parsley. Add the thyme, bay leaf, wine, oil, butter, lemon juice, and several turns of the pepper mill. Seal the foil packet: bring the 2 shorter edges of the foil together above the clams and fold them over on themselves 3 times, being careful not to squeeze the clams together; they need plenty of room inside to open. Seal the 2 sides securely. Place in the center of the oven and cook for 8 minutes. Transfer the foil packet to a large warmed ceramic serving bowl and bring to the table. Open the foil packet and serve immediately, dividing the clams and broth among 6 warmed soup plates; discard any unopened clams and the bay leaf.

oysters with a granité of their juices and sautéed chipolata sausage

SERVES 6

Begin preparations for this recipe about 5 hours before serving.

36 oysters, removed from shells and loosely wrapped in linen or cotton towel and refrigerated, juices reserved, bottom shells reserved
Juice of 1 lemon
3 shallots, minced
1 bunch chives, finely chopped
1 tablespoon sherry wine vinegar
$^1/_4$ teaspoon fine sea salt
Freshly ground black pepper
1 teaspoon mustard

3 tablespoons extra-virgin olive oil
18 tiny chipolata sausages; or 1$^1/_2$ pounds larger sausages, cut into 1$^1/_2$-inch pieces
1 sprig thyme
1 clove garlic
$^1/_4$ bunch chervil, leaves and tiny stems only, coarsely chopped
$^1/_4$ bunch tarragon, leaves and tiny stems only, coarsely chopped
$^1/_4$ bunch flat-leaf parsley, leaves and tiny stems only, coarsely chopped

Strain the juices from the oysters into a shallow metal or plastic container just large enough so that the liquid comes about $^1/_2$ inch up the side. Add the lemon juice and place in the top of the freezer for about 1 hour, until ice crystals begin to form around the edges. Remove from the freezer, scrape the edges with a fork, and stir the ice crystals into the watery center. Return to the freezer and stir the crystals about once an hour, until all the liquid has frozen and the mixture has the grainy consistency that inspired its name—*granité*—3 to 4 hours. Add the shallots and chives and stir with the fork to combine. Set aside in the freezer.

Prepare the vinaigrette: In a small bowl, combine the vinegar, salt, and 3 turns of the pepper mill. Whisk to dissolve the salt. Add the mustard and oil and whisk to emulsify; set aside.

Heat a large, nonstick skillet over medium heat. Add the sausages, thyme, and garlic clove and sauté, stirring frequently, until the sausages are browned, about 5 minutes. Transfer the sausages to a serving platter and keep warm in a low oven.

To serve, arrange 6 oyster shells around the border of each of 6 serving dishes, then place an oyster in each. Whisk the vinaigrette briefly, then combine in a bowl with the chervil, tarragon, and parsley, and toss to coat. Divide the herb salad among the six plates, placing it in the center of the dishes. Stir the *granité* well with a fork, then place about 1 teaspoon of the mixture on top of each oyster. Serve immediately, accompanied at the table by the platter of sausages.

oysters *en gelée* with shallot confit

SERVES 6

6 whole shallots, peeled
1 cup extra-virgin olive oil
1 envelope (.25 ounces) unflavored gelatin
36 oysters, removed from shells and loosely wrapped in linen or cotton towel
and refrigerated, juices reserved, bottom shells reserved
$^3/_4$ cup dry white wine
1 tablespoon minced parsley
1 lemon
$^1/_2$ teaspoon salt
1 tablespoon heavy cream
4 cups coarse sea salt or kosher salt
1 small, firm cucumber, peeled, seeded, and very finely diced
1 hard-boiled egg, yolk and white separated, yolk crushed, white very finely diced

Preheat the oven to 175° F, or the lowest setting. Spread the shallots over the bottom of a small baking dish, pour the oil over to cover the shallots well, then bake for about 1 hour, until the shallots are very tender. Transfer the shallots and oil to the bowl of a small food processor or blender and puree. Set aside.

Meanwhile, combine the gelatin with $^1/_3$ cup cold water, let stand for 2 minutes, then stir briskly to blend and partially dissolve; set aside. In a small saucepan, combine the oyster juices and the wine and heat over medium heat to hot but not boiling. Add the gelatin and the parsley and stir to combine. Transfer to a bowl and refrigerate until the gelée is chilled and well thickened but not set, 1 to 2 hours.

Squeeze the lemon juice into a small bowl, then mince the zest. Bring a small saucepan of water to a boil, add the zest and the $^1/_2$ teaspoon salt, and boil for 2 minutes. Drain well, pat dry, and set aside. Add the cream to the lemon juice and whisk to blend; set aside.

Spread the coarse sea salt on the bottom of a large platter or two smaller ones. Arrange the oyster shells on the bed of salt. Place about 1 teaspoon of the shallot puree in the bottom of each shell and top with an oyster. Sprinkle on the lemon peel, cucumber, egg yolk, and egg white evenly divided among the oysters. Spoon the lemon cream over the oysters, top with the thickened gelée, and refrigerate for 1 to 2 hours to set the gelée before serving. Bring the platter to the table and serve family-style.

mackerel and horseradish sauce, with yellow fingerling potato salad

SERVES 4

For the potato salad:
2 pounds yellow fingerling potatoes,
 scrubbed
Fine sea salt
3 small onions, minced
1 carrot, peeled and thinly sliced
3 tablespoons olive oil
1 tablespoon red-wine vinegar
2 shallots, finely chopped
1 bunch chives, chopped
Freshly ground black pepper

For the horseradish sauce:
2 tablespoons prepared mayonnaise

$1/3$ cup heavy cream
2 teaspoons prepared white horseradish
1 teaspoon sherry wine vinegar
Fine sea salt
Freshly ground black pepper

For the mackerel:
2 tablespoons unsalted butter
4 skinless mackerel fillets, about 7 ounces
 each, blotted dry
Fine sea salt
Freshly ground black pepper
1 tablespoon balsamic vinegar
Sprigs of chervil

PREPARE THE POTATO SALAD: In a pot, cover the potatoes with water, bring to a boil, and cook until the potatoes are just tender, then drain. Meanwhile, bring a pot of salted water to a boil. Add the onions and carrots and cook until tender, then drain, refresh under cold water, drain again, and blot dry. In a mixing bowl, combine the onions and carrots with the oil, red-wine vinegar, shallots, and chives, and whisk together. Add the potatoes, turning to coat with the vinaigrette, season to taste with salt and pepper, toss again, and set aside.

PREPARE THE HORSERADISH SAUCE: In a mixing bowl, combine the mayonnaise with the cream, horseradish, sherry wine vinegar, and salt and pepper to taste; stir to blend. Set aside.

PREPARE THE MACKEREL: In a heavy skillet large enough to hold the mackerel in a single layer, melt the butter over medium-high heat. Add the fillets and sauté for 5 to 6 minutes, until lightly browned. Using a spatula, carefully turn and cook the second side for the same amount of time. Remove the fillets to a platter and season with salt and pepper.

Divide the potato salad among 4 large serving plates, spooning it to one side of the plate. Place a piece of mackerel on the other side, and spoon some of the horseradish sauce around it. Decorate the plates with a light drizzle of balsamic vinegar and the chervil and serve.

lime-marinated sea scallops with dill

SERVES 6

1¼ pounds sea scallops, very thinly sliced
Fine sea salt
Freshly ground black pepper
6 tablespoons fresh lime juice
About ¾ cup extra-virgin olive oil
2 shallots, finely chopped
1 small bunch dill, leaves and tiny stems only, finely chopped

Divide the scallop slices among 6 serving plates, arranging them in overlapping concentric circles, working from the outside in. Season to taste with salt and pepper, then drizzle 1 tablespoon of the lime juice over each serving, covering the scallop slices evenly. Drizzle about 2 tablespoons of the oil over each serving, sprinkle with the shallots and dill, and serve immediately.

sea scallop salad with parmesan shavings and sherry vinaigrette

SERVES 4

For the vinaigrette:
3 tablespoons sherry wine vinegar
$^1/_4$ teaspoon fine sea salt
Freshly ground black pepper
9 tablespoons extra-virgin olive oil
2 teaspoons Dijon mustard

For the salad:
1 small head frisée
$^1/_3$ pound lamb's lettuce or mesclun
$^1/_2$ bunch chervil, leaves and tiny stems only
$^1/_2$ bunch tarragon, leaves and tiny stems only
$^1/_2$ bunch chives, sliced into $^1/_3$-inch pieces
3 small shallots, finely chopped
6 tablespoons extra-virgin olive oil
1 tablespoon finely chopped parsley
20 large sea scallops
$^1/_2$ cup balsamic vinegar
Fine sea salt
Freshly ground black pepper
3 ounces Parmesan cheese, shaved into strips

PREPARE THE VINAIGRETTE: In a small bowl, combine the sherry wine vinegar, salt, and 3 turns of the pepper mill and whisk to dissolve the salt. Add the oil and mustard and whisk to emulsify; set aside.

PREPARE THE SALAD: In a salad bowl, combine the frisée, lamb's lettuce, chervil, tarragon, chives, and shallots, toss gently to combine, and set aside. In another small bowl, combine 4 tablespoons of the oil with the parsley, stir well with a fork, and set aside.

In a large skillet, heat the remaining 2 tablespoons oil over medium heat. Add the scallops and cook for 2 minutes on each side. Transfer to a plate and set aside. Return the skillet to medium heat, add 4 tablespoons of the vinaigrette and deglaze the pan, scraping up any browned bits with a spatula or wooden spoon. Add the balsamic vinegar, stir to blend, and cook, stirring frequently, until the mixture is reduced to a thick, syrupy consistency. Season to taste with salt and pepper. Remove from the heat and set aside.

Pour the remaining vinaigrette over the salad mix and toss gently but thoroughly to coat. Spoon 1 tablespoon of the oil-parsley mixture in a ribbon around the border of each of 4 serving plates. Drizzle the reduced balsamic vinegar mixture around each plate over the olive oil mixture. Spoon a mound of the salad mixture into the center of each plate. Sprinkle the Parmesan shavings equally over each salad serving. Arrange 5 scallops around the border of each plate and serve immediately.

cold lobster with apple, avocado, and vegetable salad

SERVES 6

For the lobsters:
1 carrot, coarsely chopped
1 onion, coarsely chopped
1 bouquet garni (1 sprig thyme, 1 bay leaf, 1 sprig parsley, 1 small leek,
white and pale green parts only), tied in cheesecloth
1 cup dry white wine
2 teaspoons fine sea salt
Freshly ground black pepper
Three 2-pound lobsters

For the salad:
2 carrots, peeled and cut into $1/4$-inch cubes
1 small stalk celery, cut into $1/4$-inch cubes
1 medium potato, peeled and cut into $1/4$-inch cubes
Fine sea salt
$1/3$ pound green beans, tipped and cut into $1/4$-inch lengths
1 cup fresh baby peas or defrosted frozen baby peas
1 small crisp, red apple, peeled, cored, and cut into $1/4$-inch cubes
1 small Hass avocado, peeled, pitted, and cut into $1/4$-inch cubes
1 cup prepared mayonnaise
Freshly ground black pepper

PREPARE THE LOBSTERS: In a large, deep pot, combine the carrot, onion, bouquet garni, wine, salt, a few grinds of the pepper mill, and water. Bring to a boil over high heat and cook for 15 minutes. Add the lobsters to the pot and cook for 15 minutes more. Once the lobsters are cooked, remove the pot from the heat, let the lobsters cool to lukewarm in the cooking liquid, then remove. Using a sharp knife or scissors, split them in half lengthwise, discard the innards, and set aside, cut side down.

PREPARE THE SALAD: While the lobsters cool, in a medium pot, bring some salted water to a boil. Add the carrots, celery, and potato to the water and cook a few minutes until they are crisp-tender. Drain, plunge them into cold water to stop the cooking, drain again, and blot dry on paper towels. Transfer to a mixing bowl. Repeat the process with the green beans and peas, adding them to the bowl with the other vegetables once they are cooked and blotted dry. Add the apple and avocado to the bowl with the vegetables, and stir in $1/3$ cup of the mayonnaise, and salt and pepper to taste.

Place one of the lobster halves, cut side up, on each of 6 salad plates. Divide the vegetable salad among the plates, mounding it in the curve of the tail. Spoon a generous tablespoon of the remaining mayonnaise onto each plate next to the lobster and serve.

légumes et pâtes

VEGETABLES AND PASTA

parsleyed salsify

1 lemon, halved
2¹/₂ pounds salsify
¹/₂ cup flour
Fine sea salt
1 tablespoon unsalted butter
1 teaspoon minced garlic
2 tablespoons finely chopped flat-leaf parsley

Fill a large mixing bowl with cold water, then squeeze in the juice of the lemon, add the lemon halves, and stir to combine. Using a vegetable peeler, pare the sides of the salsify, slice them into 2-inch pieces, and immediately place them in the bowl of lemon-water as you work so that they don't discolor. Set aside.

Place the flour in a large pot, then fill slowly with 8 cups cold water, stirring with a whisk as you add the water to blend. Add about 1 teaspoon salt, stir to blend, and bring to a boil over high heat. Add the salsify, reduce the heat to medium, and cook for 30 minutes. Drain, then rinse with cool water and pat dry with paper towels.

In a medium skillet, melt the butter over medium heat. Add the salsify and cook, stirring frequently, for 4 minutes, making sure the salsify doesn't stick to the pan. Add the garlic, stir to combine, then stir in the parsley. Adjust the seasoning, transfer to a warmed serving dish, and serve immediately.

CHEF'S SUGGESTION: An autumn or winter side dish, Parsleyed Salsify are an excellent accompaniment to a variety of roasts, particularly roasted chicken or a succulent veal roast.

eggplant caviar

SERVES 6

4 small eggplants, halved lengthwise
Fine sea salt
Freshly ground black pepper
About ¹/₃ cup extra-virgin olive oil
2 sprigs thyme, halved
2 bay leaves, halved
1 medium onion, finely chopped
1 clove garlic, minced
3 medium tomatoes, peeled, seeded, and chopped
1 bouquet garni (1 sprig thyme, 1 bay leaf, 1 sprig parsley,
    1 small leek, white and green parts only), tied in cheesecloth
5 basil leaves, finely julienned

Preheat the oven to 350° F. Sprinkle the cut sides of the eggplants with a generous pinch of salt and several turns of the pepper mill. Drizzle about 1 teaspoon oil over each cut side, then place ¹/₂ sprig thyme and ¹/₂ bay leaf on one half of each sliced eggplant. Press the two halves of each eggplant back together, enclosing the thyme and bay leaf, and wrap each tightly in a sheet of aluminum foil. Bake for 35 minutes. Cool for a few minutes, then unwrap and scoop out the flesh of the eggplants. Place in a strainer to drain out excess liquid, then chop finely and set aside.

Meanwhile, in a medium skillet, heat 3 tablespoons oil over medium heat. Add the onion and garlic and cook, stirring frequently, for 3 to 4 minutes, until the onion softens and begins to look transparent. Add the tomatoes, bouquet garni, and a generous pinch of salt and several turns of the pepper mill and stir to combine. Reduce the heat to medium-low and simmer, stirring frequently, for 15 minutes. Add the eggplant, stir to incorporate, and cook for 2 minutes. Stir in the basil and remove from the heat. Set the pan on a wire rack to cool, then serve at room temperature. Or, refrigerate for several hours and serve chilled.

CHEF'S SUGGESTION: Serve accompanied by slices of toasted baguette or country bread. You can also serve Eggplant Caviar as a hot appetizer: after adding the basil and removing from the heat, spread the mixture into a small baking dish, and sprinkle about ¹/₂ cup freshly grated Parmesan cheese evenly over the top. Place under the broiler until the top browns. Serve immediately.

fried zucchini blossoms

SERVES 6

1¹/₂ cups flour
2 envelopes (5 ounces) active dry yeast
1¹/₂ cups beer, at room temperature
4 cups vegetable oil
36 zucchini blossoms, pistils snipped off
Fine sea salt
Freshly ground black pepper

In a mixing bowl, combine the flour and the yeast and stir to blend. Add the beer a little at a time, stirring constantly with a wooden spoon to obtain a smooth, lump-free batter. Set aside for 10 minutes.

In a deep-fryer or a heavy, 2-quart saucepan, heat the oil over medium-high heat to 315°–325° F. The oil should be no hotter or the blossoms will fry too quickly and will burn. Working in 7 or 8 batches, dip each blossom into the batter, coating it well, then carefully place in the fryer. When the blossoms are golden and crisp, remove and drain on several layers of paper towels and season with salt and pepper. Repeat with the remaining blossoms. Serve hot.

CHEF'S SUGGESTION: Zucchini blossoms are a great delicacy of the late spring and summer. If you don't grow your own, you may be able to find them in season at a good farmer's market. Serve Fried Zucchini Blossoms as an hors d'oeuvre with *aperitifs*, or as a first course accompanied by a tartar sauce (combine 1 cup mayonnaise or 1 cup whipped crème fraîche with 5 minced gherkins, 1 teaspoon Dijon mustard, 1 tablespoon minced capers, and 1 tablespoon minced fresh green herbs).

endive gratin with ham

For the endives:
6 endives, bottoms trimmed
Juice of 1 lemon
About 7 tablespoons (3½ ounces) unsalted butter
1 teaspoon sugar
Fine sea salt
3 slices baked ham

For the béchamel sauce:
4 tablespoons unsalted butter
⅓ cup flour
3 cups milk
1⅓ cups (about 4 ounces) grated Gruyère cheese
Fine sea salt

PREPARE THE ENDIVES: Preheat the oven to 450° F. In a small ceramic baking dish, combine the endives, 1 cup water, and the lemon juice. Cut 4 tablespoons of the butter into bits and scatter them over the endives, then sprinkle on the sugar and a pinch of salt. Cut a piece of kitchen parchment just large enough to cover the endives inside the pan. Rub one side with about 1 teaspoon butter and place butter side down over the endives. Bake for 40 minutes, then drain off excess liquid, lightly pressing the endives, and set aside.

MEANWHILE, PREPARE THE BÉCHAMEL SAUCE: In a heavy-bottom saucepan, melt the butter over medium heat. Add the flour and whisk to blend. Slowly pour in the milk, whisking constantly to incorporate. Bring mixture to a boil, then reduce the heat to maintain a simmer and cook, stirring frequently, for about 5 minutes, until the sauce is thick and creamy. Add three-quarters of the cheese and a generous pinch of salt and stir to blend. When the cheese has melted into the sauce, remove from the heat and set aside.

Preheat the oven to 450° F. Wrap each endive in a slice of ham. Butter a porcelain gratin dish or baking dish with 1 tablespoon of the butter, then place the endives in the dish and spoon over the béchamel sauce. Sprinkle on the remaining cheese, cut the remaining 1½ tablespoons or so of butter into bits and dot them over the top. Bake for about 3 minutes, until the top is browned and bubbly. Serve immediately.

broccoli and cauliflower gratin with ham

SERVES 4

Fine sea salt
1 pound broccoli, florets only
1 pound cauliflower, florets only
4 tablespoons unsalted butter
$^1/_3$ cup flour
2 cups milk
4 egg yolks
1$^1/_3$ cups (about 4 ounces) grated Gruyère cheese
Freshly ground black pepper
Freshly grated nutmeg
$^1/_2$ pound baked ham, finely diced
$^1/_2$ cup fine bread crumbs

Bring a large pot of water to a boil over high heat. Add about 1 teaspoon salt, the broccoli, and cauliflower. Blanch for 1 minute, then drain and set aside.

Preheat the oven to 400° F. In a heavy-bottom saucepan, melt 3 tablespoons of the butter over medium heat. Add the flour and whisk to blend. Slowly pour in the milk, whisking constantly to incorporate. Bring to a boil, stirring constantly, and cook, still stirring constantly, for about 5 minutes, until the sauce has thickened. Remove the pan from the heat and, one by one, add the egg yolks and whisk to incorporate. Add the cheese, salt and pepper to taste, and a pinch of nutmeg and stir to incorporate, then remove from the heat.

Coat the bottom and sides of a large porcelain baking dish with the remaining 1 tablespoon butter. Arrange the broccoli, cauliflower, and ham in alternating layers in the baking dish, first a layer of broccoli, then cauliflower, then ham. Spoon the sauce over the mixture, then sprinkle on the remaining cheese and the bread crumbs. Bake for about 30 minutes, until the top is richly browned and bubbly. Serve immediately.

potato gratin

ı clove garlic, halved
^{1}/₂ cup unsalted butter
2 pounds Idaho potatoes, peeled and very thinly sliced
ı^1/₃ cups (about 4 ounces) grated Gruyère cheese
Fine sea salt
Freshly ground black pepper
^{1}/₈ teaspoon freshly grated nutmeg
ı cup heavy cream
ı cup milk

Preheat the oven to 400 ° F. Rub the garlic generously over the bottom and sides of a large, shallow porcelain gratin dish or shallow baking dish, then coat with about ı^1/₂ tablespoons of the butter. Arrange one-third of the potatoes over the bottom of the plate in a single layer, the potato slices slightly overlapping each other. Top with one-third of the cheese. Sprinkle generously with salt and pepper, and a pinch of nutmeg. Repeat twice with the remaining potatoes, finishing the top with the remaining cheese. In a small mixing bowl, combine the cream and milk and beat to blend. Pour over the potatoes. Bake in the center of the oven for 50 minutes, then remove from the oven. If the top isn't a rich, golden brown, place under the broiler for a minute or two, until the top attains the desired color. Serve immediately.

potato cake darphin

2¹/₂ pounds waxy eastern (Maine) potatoes, peeled and grated
into ¹/₄-inch strips
Fine sea salt
Freshly ground black pepper
¹/₂ cup peanut oil
1 tablespoon unsalted butter, cut into small bits

Preheat the oven to 325° F. Just before cooking, pat the potato strips very dry with paper towels to remove all excess moisture, then generously sprinkle with salt and pepper. Heat the oil in a large, nonstick, oven-proof skillet over medium-high heat. Add the potatoes and, using a spatula, press down into an even layer, then form them into a large, flat pancake. Raise the heat to high, evenly dot the butter over the top, and cook for 3 to 4 minutes, until the bottom is browned and crusty. Remove from the heat.

With the help of a spatula, slide the pancake onto a large dinner plate, cover with another large dinner plate, flip it over, then gently slide it back into the skillet to brown on the other side. Return to high heat and cook for 3 to 4 minutes, until browned and crusty. Transfer to the oven and bake for 10 minutes. Cut the pancake into 6 wedges and serve immediately.

eggplant stuffed with tomato, basil, parmesan, and ham

SERVES 6

6 small eggplants, halved lengthwise
6 tablespoons extra-virgin olive oil
Fine sea salt
Freshly ground black pepper
2 red-ripe tomatoes
1 medium onion, finely chopped
1 medium zucchini, finely diced
1 red bell pepper, finely diced
12 basil leaves, finely julienned
1 cup (about 4 ounces) freshly grated Parmesan cheese
3 eggs, lightly beaten
6 thin slices (about ¼ pound) boiled ham, finely julienned
About 1 teaspoon thyme blossoms or thyme leaves

Preheat the oven to 400° F. Using a small, sharp knife, cut a shallow cross-hatch pattern into the cut side of each eggplant half, place cut side up on a baking sheet, then drizzle each with 1 teaspoon oil. Sprinkle with salt and pepper and bake for 10 minutes, or until they are browned and tender to the touch. Set aside on a wire rack.

Fill a large saucepan with water and bring to a boil. Plunge the tomatoes into the boiling water for 1 minute then immediately transfer to a bowl of cold water; this will loosen the skin. Using a paring knife, gently remove the skin, then coarsely chop the tomatoes and set aside.

In a large skillet, heat 2 tablespoons of the oil over medium heat. Add the onion and cook, stirring frequently, until softened and slightly translucent, about 4 minutes. Add the tomatoes, season with salt and pepper to taste, and cook, stirring frequently, for 10 minutes. Transfer to a bowl and set aside. Heat ı tablespoon of the oil in the skillet over medium-high heat, add the zucchini and pepper, and cook, stirring frequently, until the vegetables color and soften slightly, about 3 minutes. Transfer to the bowl with the tomato mixture.

Gently scoop out the flesh of the eggplants, taking care not to tear the skin, and place in a mixing bowl. Add the tomato mixture, basil, cheese, eggs, and ham. Season with salt and pepper to taste, add the remaining ı tablespoon oil, and stir well with a wooden spoon to combine. Arrange the eggplant shells in a large, shallow, greased baking pan. Divide the vegetable mixture among the 12 shells, gently mounding each portion. Sprinkle each with a pinch of thyme blossoms, then bake for 7 to 10 minutes, until the stuffing is lightly browned and heated through. Serve immediately.

CHEF'S SUGGESTION: These stuffed eggplants are delicious served with a tossed salad of greens and fresh green herbs. The combination makes an excellent lunch dish. In the summer you could also serve the eggplants chilled as an appetizer.

tagliatelle with asparagus and smoked salmon

SERVES 6

1½ pounds thin green asparagus, peeled, tough root ends trimmed
Fine sea salt
6 tablespoons unsalted butter
1 onion, grated
¼ cup sherry
1 cup crème fraîche
3 tablespoons finely chopped chives
About 1¾ cups (4½ ounces) grated Parmesan cheese
¼ pound thinly sliced smoked salmon, cut into ¼-inch strips
Freshly ground black pepper
1 pound fresh tagliatelle

Place the asparagus in a large pot of cold water. Add about 1 teaspoon salt and bring to a boil over high heat. Cook until the asparagus are just tender, but not soft, about 5 or 6 minutes. (The cooking time of asparagus can vary according to their thickness, so watch them carefully so they do not overcook). Drain them, then plunge them immediately into very cold water to stop the cooking. Slice off the asparagus tips on the bias and set aside; slice the stems on the bias into 1½-inch pieces and set aside.

In a medium skillet, melt the butter over medium heat. Add the asparagus stems and the onion and stir to combine. Cook, stirring frequently, for 1 minute, then cover and cook for 2 minutes. Uncover, add the sherry, and cook for 3 minutes, stirring occasionally, to allow the alcohol in the sherry to evaporate. Add the crème fraîche, stir to combine, then cook until the cream is on the brink of boiling. Remove from the heat, then add the asparagus tips, chives, ¼ cup of the cheese, the salmon, and ¼ teaspoon salt and ¼ teaspoon pepper, stir gently to combine, and set aside.

Bring a large pot of salted water to a boil over high heat. Add the pasta and cook for about 1 minute, or until just tender. Drain, then transfer to a large, warmed bowl, combine with the asparagus-salmon sauce, and gently toss to combine. Divide among 6 warmed serving bowls or plates, sprinkle each serving with about 2 teaspoons of the cheese, and serve immediately, accompanied by the remaining cheese on the side.

pasta with pesto and shellfish

SERVES 6

1 cup small basil leaves, loosely packed
3 cloves garlic, peeled, quartered lengthwise, and crushed
2 ounces (about $^1/_3$ cup) pine nuts, crushed
about $^1/_2$ cup (2 ounces) grated Parmesan cheese
4 ounces grated Comté or Gruyère cheese
$^1/_2$ cup extra-virgin olive oil
1 tablespoon unsalted butter
5 medium shallots, finely chopped
$^1/_2$ pound baby clams, shells scrubbed
$^1/_2$ pound mussels, shells scrubbed
$^1/_2$ pound cockles, shells scrubbed
2 sprigs flat-leaf parsley
1 sprig thyme
1 bay leaf
$^1/_2$ cup dry white wine
1 pound fresh linguine pasta
Fleur de sel or coarse sea salt

In the bowl of a small food processor, or by hand with a mortar and pestle, process or mash the basil to form a puree. Add the garlic and process or mash to blend, then add the pine nuts and process or mash to blend. Transfer to a mixing bowl, add the cheeses, and stir to combine. Using all but 2 tablespoons of the oil, slowly drizzle a thin stream into the bowl, whisking constantly at the same time. Whisk until the mixture is a smooth, dense paste. Set the pesto aside.

In a large saucepan, melt the butter over medium heat. Add the shallots and cook, stirring frequently, until the shallots soften, about 3 minutes. Add the clams, mussels, cockles, parsley, thyme, and bay leaf, then pour in the wine and bring to a boil over medium-high heat. Cook just until the shells open; with a slotted spoon, remove shellfish from heat and set aside until cool enough to handle; discard any unopened shells. Reduce the cooking liquid by half and set aside. Separate 6 clams, 6 mussels, and 6 cockles in their shells and reserve for garnish; then remove the remaining clams, mussels, and cockles from their shells and set aside.

Bring a large pot of salted water to a boil over high heat. Add the pasta and cook until tender. Drain, then transfer to a large warmed serving platter. Add the cooking liquid and toss gently. Add the pesto and toss gently to coat the pasta. Scatter the shellfish over the top, drizzle with the remaining 2 tablespoons oil, garnish each plate with one each of the reserved clams, mussels, and cockles still in their shells, sprinkle with the fleur de sel, and serve immediately.

bow-tie pasta with clam sauce

SERVES 4

Fine sea salt
1 1/2 pounds clams, shells scrubbed
1/2 cup dry white wine
1 shallot, finely chopped
1 clove garlic, minced
4 tablespoons extra-virgin olive oil
1 tablespoon unsalted butter
10 ounces (about 7 1/2 cups) bow-tie pasta
2 tablespoons finely chopped parsley

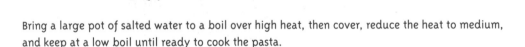

Bring a large pot of salted water to a boil over high heat, then cover, reduce the heat to medium, and keep at a low boil until ready to cook the pasta.

In a large saucepan, combine the clams, wine, shallot, garlic, and 2 tablespoons of the oil and bring just to a boil over medium heat. Cover and cook just until the calms open. Using a slotted spoon, transfer the clams to a bowl as they open, discarding any that haven't opened. Pour the cooking liquid through a fine strainer—leaving behind any sand and other residue—into a clean saucepan. Bring to a boil over medium heat, add the butter, and stir to blend. When the butter is completely melted, remove from the heat and set aside.

Add the remaining 2 tablespoons oil to the pot of boiling water, then bring the water to a rolling bowl over high heat. Meanwhile, remove the clams from their shells, discard the shells, and reserve the clams. Add the pasta to the water and cook until al dente, or just tender. Immediately add some cold water to the pot to stop the cooking, and drain. Transfer the pasta to a warmed serving platter, add the sauce and the clams and toss gently to combine. Sprinkle with parsley and serve immediately.

muenster ravioli

SERVES 6

$3/4$ pound Muenster cheese, cut into $1/2$-inch cubes
$1/3$ cup finely chopped parsley
1 pound fresh pasta sheets, cut into 2-inch squares
Fine sea salt
1 cup chicken stock
2 tablespoons extra-virgin olive oil
2 medium tomatoes, diced
$2/3$ cup whole basil leaves, loosely packed

Place the cheese and parsley in a mixing bowl and toss to combine. On half of the pasta squares place a cube of Muenster and some parsley bits. Cover each square with another pasta square and press around the edges to close. You should have 30 to 36 ravioli; if there are more, refrigerate or freeze the extras for another time.

Bring a large pot of salted water to a boil over high heat. Add the ravioli and cook for 5 minutes. Meanwhile, heat the stock in a microwave oven or in a small saucepan on the stove and set aside. Carefully pour the ravioli into a colander to drain.

Arrange 5 or 6 ravioli on each of 6 warmed serving plates. Drizzle the chicken stock and 1 teaspoon oil over each serving, add the tomatoes, garnish with the basil, and serve immediately.

lasagna salad with sautéed squid and parmesan shavings in sherry vinaigrette

SERVES 6

3 large, very ripe tomatoes
Fine sea salt
Freshly ground black pepper
1 cup extra-virgin olive oil
3 tablespoons sherry vinegar
1 tablespoon Dijon mustard
1 pound fresh lasagna pasta, cut into twelve 4-inch squares
3/4 pound squid, cleaned, rinsed in cold water, well drained, and cut into thin rings
Juice of 1 lemon
12 basil leaves
18 oil-cured black olives, pitted and coarsely chopped
1/4 pound Parmesan cheese, sliced into thin shavings with a
vegetable peeler or mandoline slicer

Preheat the oven to 220° F. Bring a large pot of water to boil over high heat. Drop in the tomatoes and cook for 10 seconds. Remove with a slotted spoon, plunge them into a bowl of ice water, let cool for about 20 seconds, then transfer to paper towels and dry. Peel off the skin, cut the tomatoes into quarters, then remove and discard the seeds. Arrange the pieces on a baking sheet, season with salt and pepper and drizzle with 1 tablespoon of the oil; place in the center of the oven and bake for 15 minutes. Transfer the tomato pieces to a plate and set aside in the refrigerator.

To prepare the vinaigrette, combine the vinegar with a pinch of salt in a small bowl and whisk to dissolve the salt. Add several turns of the pepper mill, the mustard, and 3/4 cup of the oil and whisk to emulsify. Set aside.

Bring a large pot of lightly salted water to a boil over high heat. Add the pasta squares and cook for about 3 minutes, until they are just tender. Remove with a slotted spoon and plunge immediately into a bowl of ice water to stop the cooking. Transfer to a clean cotton or linen towel to drain. Set aside.

In a skillet, heat the remaining 3 tablespoons oil over medium heat. Add the squid and sauté just until the squid turns white, 2 to 3 minutes; be careful not to overcook, since the squid can quickly become tough. Remove from the heat, sprinkle with the lemon juice, stir to incorporate, then transfer to a plate and set aside.

Arrange 2 pasta squares in the center of each of 6 serving plates, one slightly overlapping the other. Garnish each with the sautéed squid, 2 pieces of tomato, 2 basil leaves, and the chopped olives. Drizzle on the vinaigrette, scatter the cheese over, and serve.

coquillages et poissons

SHELLFISH AND FISH

roasted bay scallops
with chive butter

SERVES 6

$^3/_4$ pound coarse sea salt or kosher salt
2 pounds bay scallops
$^1/_2$ cup salted butter, softened
2 shallots, finely chopped
1 small bunch chives, finely chopped
Juice of 1 small lemon
Fine sea salt
Freshly ground black pepper

Preheat the oven to 400° F. Spread the coarse salt over a serving plate, then place the scallops atop the salt. Set aside for 15 minutes; this firms the texture of the scallops and removes excess liquid. Meanwhile, place the butter in a small bowl, add the shallots, chives, lemon juice, and salt and pepper to taste, and mix to blend all the ingredients.

Arrange the scallops in a ceramic baking dish or a baking pan. Top each scallop with about 1 teaspoon of the butter mixture. Bake in the top third of the oven for 5 to 7 minutes, until the scallops turn light golden brown and the butter is bubbly. Serve immediately.

sautéed scallops with endives and bitter-orange butter

SERVES 6

4 to 5 tablespoons unsalted butter, chilled, plus 8 tablespoons unsalted butter, melted
2 pounds endives, leaves separated, washed in cold water and patted dry
$^1/_4$ cup bitter-orange juice (juice of 6 small bitter oranges);
if unavailable, use $^1/_4$ cup orange juice
$1^1/_2$ pounds scallops
Fine sea salt
Freshly ground black pepper
1 small bunch dill

In a large skillet, melt 3 tablespoons of the chilled butter over medium heat. Add the endives, stir to coat with the butter, then sprinkle the sugar over the endives. Cook, stirring frequently, until the endives soften and lightly caramelize, about 8 minutes.

Deglaze the pan with the orange juice, stirring to combine, and scraping up any browned bits stuck to the pan. Using a slotted spoon, transfer the endives to a bowl; keep warm in a very low oven. Pour the orange juice–butter mixture from the pan into a separate bowl. Add the melted butter and whisk until the sauce emulsifies; season to taste with salt and pepper, then keep warm in the oven.

Heat a nonstick skillet over medium-high heat, or melt 1 tablespoon of the butter in a traditional skillet over medium-high heat. Add the scallops, season to taste with salt and pepper, and sauté quickly, just until the scallops are cooked through and lightly browned, about 3 minutes. Drain any accumulated juice from the endives, and divide them among 6 warmed serving plates. Divide the scallops equally among the plates, arranging them on top of the endives. Drizzle the orange-butter sauce over and around the scallops, garnish with small sprigs of dill, and serve immediately.

red snapper with harissa, and figs roasted with sesame seeds

SERVES 6

For the figs:
6 firm, ripe figs
1 tablespoon clarified butter
1 tablespoon sesame seeds, lightly toasted

For the couscous:
1½ cups (about ½ pound) medium-grain instant couscous
3 tablespoons extra-virgin olive oil
1/2 bunch fresh mint, leaves only, cut into thin strips
½ red bell pepper, finely diced
1 medium tomato, finely diced

For the pesto:
½ bunch fresh basil, leaves only, chopped
2 cloves garlic, minced
6 tablespoons extra-virgin olive oil

For the red snapper:
8 tablespoons unsalted butter, softened
½ cup freshly grated Parmesan cheese
3 tablespoons fresh bread crumbs
2 tablespoons harissa
1 tablespoon olive oil
12 red snapper fillets, about 3 ounces each, blotted dry

PREPARE THE FIGS: In a medium skillet, cook the figs in the clarified butter over medium heat for 3 minutes, turning once or twice. Sprinkle the sesame seeds over and set aside.

PREPARE THE COUSCOUS: Following the package directions, put the couscous in a heatproof bowl, add the appropriate amount of boiling water and the oil, and let it sit until all of the liquid has been absorbed. Stir in the mint, red pepper, and tomato. Season to taste with salt and pepper and set aside.

PREPARE THE PESTO: In the bowl of a food processor, combine the basil and garlic, and pulse to blend. Add the oil and process until smoothly pureed. Set aside.

PREPARE THE RED SNAPPER: Preheat the oven to 400° F. In a medium bowl, combine the butter, cheese, bread crumbs, and harissa, and whisk until smoothly blended. Brush the red snapper fillets with a little oil, place them on a baking sheet, and bake for 3 minutes. Spread on the harissa-butter mixture and bake for 2 minutes more, or until lightly browned.

Divide the couscous among 6 warmed serving plates, mounding it in the center. Place two fillets on each serving of couscous. Drizzle a ribbon of pesto over the fish, garnish each plate with a fig, and serve.

stuffed tomatoes with skate, shallots, and herbs

SERVES 6

2 tablespoons white-wine vinegar
2 sprigs thyme
2 bay leaves
1 skate wing, about 1^1/3 pounds
2 tablespoons red-wine vinegar
Fine sea salt
Freshly ground black pepper
6 tablespoons extra-virgin olive oil
6 red-ripe medium tomatoes
3 shallots, finely chopped
1 bunch chives, finely chopped
1 bunch chervil, leaves and tiny sprigs only,
   finely chopped
1 small bunch basil, leaves only, finely chopped
^{1}/2 pound baby spinach
1^1/2 cups freshly made croutons (dice country bread small
   and sauté in butter until crisp)

Fill a fish poacher, or a large deep skillet, with enough water to come just below the poaching rack. Add the white-wine vinegar, thyme, and bay leaves, and bring to a boil over medium-high heat. Reduce the heat to medium-low, so that the water just simmers, then add the skate. Cover the poacher or skillet and cook for about 15 minutes, until the fish is cooked through. Remove from the heat, transfer the skate to a platter, and, when it's cool enough to handle, remove the skin from both sides and set aside.

MAKE THE VINAIGRETTE: in a small bowl, combine the red-wine vinegar with a generous pinch of salt and 7 or 8 turns of the pepper mill, and stir until salt dissolves. Add the oil and whisk to emulsify; set aside.

Cut the top third off the tomatoes and scoop out the core and seeds and discard. Season the interiors of the tomatoes with salt and pepper, and set aside.

Flake the skate into a mixing bowl. Add the shallots, chives, chervil, and basil and, using a wooden spoon, stir to combine. Add the vinaigrette and stir to incorporate. Stuff the tomatoes with the skate filling, mounding it above the tops of the tomatoes. Arrange the baby spinach over the bottoms of six salad plates, then place a tomato in the center of each. Sprinkle the croutons over the tomatoes and spinach, and serve immediately.

hake crusted with coarse pepper, and polenta with olives

SERVES 10

2 cups milk
1 teaspoon salt
$^1/_2$ cup polenta
$^3/_4$ cup extra-virgin olive oil
4 ounces (about 1 cup) Niçoise olives, pitted and coarsely chopped
10 hake (whiting) fillets, about 6 ounces each
3 teaspoons coarsely ground black pepper
Fine sea salt
2 bunches chervil, leaves and tiny stems only, coarsely chopped
2 bunches tarragon, leaves and tiny stems only, coarsely chopped
2 bunches chives, chopped
2 bunches dill, leaves and tiny stems only, coarsely chopped
2 tablespoons sherry wine vinegar
8 tablespoons olive oil
Freshly ground black pepper

Bring the milk and salt to a boil. Add the polenta in a slow steady stream, stirring constantly, and cook over medium-low heat for 30 minutes. Stir in $^1/_3$ cup of the oil and the olives, and spread the polenta on a lightly oiled jelly roll pan to a thickness of $^1/_4$ inch. Let it set, then cut it into neat rectangles. Preheat the broiler. Brush the polenta rectangles with a little more oil, then broil briefly, until the polenta is lightly browned. Keep warm.

In a large skillet, heat 3 tablespoons of the oil over medium heat. Coat the hake fillets with the coarse pepper, place in the skillet, and sauté until golden brown, 3 to 4 minutes, turning once. Season with salt. In a mixing bowl, combine the chervil, tarragon, chives, and dill. Add the vinegar, the remaining 5 tablespoons oil, and salt and pepper to taste, and toss well to combine.

Place a rectangle of polenta in the center of 10 warmed serving plates and place a hake fillet on each. Divide the herb salad among the plates, drizzle a thin ribbon of oil over each fillet, and serve.

cod fillets with chorizo scales and white bean puree

SERVES 6

For the bean puree:
3/4 pound (1 1/2 cups) Great Northern beans, soaked overnight and rinsed
1 carrot, peeled
1 onion, studded with 1 clove
1 large potato, peeled and coarsely chopped
2 ounces slab bacon, cut into pieces
1 bouquet garni (1 sprig thyme, 1 bay leaf, 1 sprig parsley, 1 small leek,
white and pale green parts only), tied in cheesecloth
4 cups rich chicken stock
8 tablespoons unsalted butter
2 tablespoons sherry wine vinegar
Fine sea salt
Freshly ground black pepper

For the brown butter sauce:
1 cup rich chicken stock
1 cup unsalted butter
2 tablespoons sherry wine vinegar
Fine sea salt
Freshly ground black pepper

For the cod:
8 ounces chorizo, casings removed and thinly sliced
6 center-cut cod fillets, about 6 ounces each
1 egg yolk, beaten
Fine sea salt
Freshly ground black pepper
3 tablespoons olive oil

PREPARE THE BEAN PUREE: Combine the beans, carrot, onion, potato, bacon, and bouquet garni in a large pot. Add the stock, bring to a simmer, and cook for 45 to 50 minutes, until the beans are soft. Strain and discard the carrot, onion, bacon, and bouquet garni. Return the beans and potato to the pot. Add the butter, and using a fork, mash the beans and potatoes until almost smooth. Stir in the vinegar, season with salt and pepper to taste, and keep warm in a low oven.

PREPARE THE BROWN BUTTER SAUCE: In a small saucepan, cook the stock over high heat until it is reduced by three-quarters. In a skillet over medium heat, melt the butter and cook until it is light brown. Stir in the vinegar, then whisk in the reduced stock. Season with salt and pepper, and keep warm in the top of a double boiler until ready to serve.

PREPARE THE COD: Bring a small pot of water to a boil. Add the chorizo slices, cook for 1 minute, then drain and plunge them into cold water. Drain and blot dry on paper towels. Lightly brush the tops of the cod fillets with egg yolk. Season with salt and pepper and arrange the chorizo slices on top of each fillet in an overlapping pattern like fish scales.

Preheat the oven to 450° F. In a large, nonstick, ovenproof skillet, heat enough oil to liberally cover the bottom of the pan and place over medium-high heat. Using two spatulas to hold the chorizo slices on the fillets, place the fillets, chorizo side down, in the skillet and sauté for 5 or 6 seconds. Again using two spatulas, carefully turn the fish, adjust the heat to medium-low, and cook for 5 minutes. Transfer the pan to the oven and cook for 3 to 4 minutes.

Place a cod fillet in the center of each of 6 warmed dinner plates, rearranging the scales if necessary. Divide the puree among the plates, spoon the sauce over the fish, and serve.

sautéed fillet of striped bass with sorrel, capers, and anchovies

SERVES 6

Six ^{1}/2-pound fillets striped bass
Fine sea salt
Freshly ground black pepper
About ^{1}/3 cup extra-virgin olive oil
2 bunches sorrel, well washed in cold water, trimmed
1 tablespoon capers
Juice of 1 lemon
12 anchovy fillets

Generously season the bass fillets with salt and pepper and set aside for 30 minutes.

In a large skillet, heat 2 to 3 tablespoons of the oil over medium heat. Reduce the heat to medium-low and add the bass fillets (work in batches if necessary). Sauté the fillets for 2 to 3 minutes on each side, until the fillets are just cooked through. Transfer to a warmed platter and keep warm in a low oven. Add the remaining oil and heat over medium-high heat. Add the sorrel and sauté, stirring frequently, for 1 minute. Add the capers, stir to combine, and cook, stirring frequently, for about 30 seconds. Remove from the heat. Divide the sorrel mixture among 6 warmed serving plates. Place a bass fillet on top of each serving of sorrel, sprinkle generously with the lemon juice, garnish with 2 anchovy fillets each, and serve immediately.

crumb-topped sea bass with sautéed pears, lemon zest, and baby spinach salad

SERVES 4

1 tablespoon sherry wine vinegar
Fine sea salt
Freshly ground black pepper
3 tablespoons plus a bit more for garnish extra-virgin olive oil
$1/3$ pound baby spinach, rinsed
1 shallot, finely chopped
2 tablespoons unsalted butter, chilled; plus 6 tablespoons melted
1 pear, ripe but firm, peeled, cored, and finely diced
Zest of $1/2$ lemon, minced
Zest of $1/2$ orange, minced
Four center-cut sea bass fillets, about 6 ounces each
2 cups very coarse unseasoned bread crumbs, preferably fresh (in a food processor or by
hand, coarsely chop 4 slices dense white bread, then dry for 1 hour in 200° F oven)
1 tablespoon finely chopped parsley
About 1 tablespoon balsamic vinegar
$1/4$ cup chopped toasted almonds
About 1 tablespoon maple syrup, optional

In a small bowl, combine the sherry vinegar with $1/8$ teaspoon fine sea salt and 3 or 4 turns of the pepper mill and whisk to dissolve the salt. Add 3 tablespoons of the oil and whisk to emulsify. Set the vinaigrette aside. In a salad bowl, combine the spinach and the shallot, toss gently to combine, and set aside.

In a small skillet, melt the 2 tablespoons chilled butter over medium heat. Add the pear, stir to combine, and cook, stirring frequently, until the pear takes on a pale golden color, about 4 minutes. Stir in the lemon and orange zests, then remove from the heat and set aside in the pan.

Season the bass fillets with salt and pepper. Dip 1 side into the melted butter, coating it well, then press that side of each fillet into the bread crumbs, coating the surface evenly. In a large skillet, heat 2 tablespoons of the leftover melted butter over medium heat. Using two spatulas to hold the fillets, carefully place each fillet in the skillet breaded side down and cook for 4 minutes. Again using two spatulas, carefully turn the fillets, reduce the heat to low, and cook for 5 minutes. Remove from the heat and set aside in the pan.

Pour the vinaigrette over the spinach and shallot and toss gently to coat well. Divide the salad among 4 serving plates, mounding the salad in the center of each plate. Place a fillet on top of each mound of spinach. Spoon the pear mixture and the parsley around the fillets, then drizzle each serving of pear with a few drops of balsamic vinegar and a thin trickle of the remaining oil. Scatter the almonds over each plate, sprinkle a few drops of maple syrup on the fish, if you want, and serve immediately.

baked whitefish in salt crust

2 cups rye flour
^{2}/3 cup cornmeal
8 to 10 egg whites
1 cup fine sea salt, plus additional for seasoning
1 whole whitefish, about 3^1/2 to 4 pounds, scaled, gilled, gutted,
and tail removed, blotted dry
2 large sprigs dill, plus 2 tablespoons chopped dill
6 thin slices pork fatback, about 4 by 6 inches each
1 shallot, chopped
1 cup good-quality fish stock
3 tablespoons dry white wine
^{3}/4 cup heavy cream
2 tablespoons unsalted butter
1 tablespoon minced anchovy fillets in oil
Freshly ground black pepper

In a medium mixing bowl, blend the rye flour, cornmeal, 8 egg whites, and salt into a smooth pastry. If the mixture is dry, add another egg white or two until it forms a smooth dough. Form into a ball, cover with plastic wrap, and refrigerate for 30 minutes.

Lightly season inside of the whitefish with salt. Lay the dill sprigs inside the fish and cover the fish completely with the fatback.

Remove the dough from the refrigerator. On a lightly floured board, using a floured rolling pin, roll the pastry into a long oval shape, large enough to amply cover the fish, about ^{1}/4 inch thick. Place the fish on one side of the pastry, near the center. Wrap the pastry around the fish, pressing to seal the seams. It should stick together easily.

Preheat the oven to 450° F. Line a baking sheet with parchment paper and place the whitefish on it. Bake for 30 minutes.

Meanwhile, in a small saucepan, combine the shallot, stock, and wine. Cook over high heat until the liquid is reduced to the consistency of a thick syrup. Add the cream and cook until it thickens slightly. Stir in the butter and the anchovies, with a little of their oil, then scrape the mixture into an electric blender and purée until smooth. Strain the sauce into a small saucepan, stir in the dill, and season to taste with pepper. Keep warm until ready to serve. *Do not let it return to a boil.*

Remove the fish from the oven. At the table, cut off the top of the crust and remove the fatback covering. Serve each portion of fish with a generous spoonful of anchovy sauce.

CHEF'S SUGGESTION: The fish and sauce go well with plain boiled potatoes. To easily cut fatback into very thin slices, freeze it for 15 to 30 minutes before cutting. Or ask the deli department in your food store to slice it on their electric slicer.

nut-crusted baked salmon with lamb's lettuce salad

SERVES 6

For the salmon:
1 cup unsalted butter, softened, plus 2 to 3 tablespoons
Fine sea salt
Freshly ground black pepper
1/2 bunch rosemary, leaves only, finely chopped
3 1/2 ounces finely chopped walnuts
3 1/2 ounces finely chopped hazelnuts
1/2 cup unseasoned bread crumbs
6 salmon fillets, about 6 ounces each

For the salad:
1 tablespoon red-wine vinegar
3 tablespoons extra-virgin olive oil
2 shallots, finely chopped
1/2 pound lamb's lettuce or mixed baby greens

PREPARE THE SALMON: In a small mixing bowl, combine the butter and generous pinches of salt and pepper. Add the rosemary and nuts and stir to blend, then stir in the bread crumbs. Set aside.

Preheat the oven to 425° F. In a large skillet, melt 2 tablespoons butter over medium heat. Working in batches, add the salmon fillets and cook for 2 minutes on each side (add 1 more tablespoon of butter to the pan if necessary). Transfer the fillets to a lightly buttered baking sheet. Divide the rosemary-nut topping among the 6 fillets, pressing the mixture gently onto the top of each fillet to cover evenly. Bake in the center of the oven for 3 minutes.

MEANWHILE, MAKE THE SALAD: In a small bowl, combine the vinegar with a pinch of salt and several turns of the pepper mill and whisk to dissolve the salt. Add the oil and shallots and whisk to emulsify. Place the lamb's lettuce in a salad bowl, pour in the vinaigrette, and toss to coat well.

Place a salmon fillet in the center of each of 6 serving plates. Arrange the salad decoratively around the salmon and serve immediately.

sautéed monkfish and bacon brochettes with caper-cornichon mayonnaise

SERVES 6

3/4 cup mayonnaise
7 tablespoons capers, well-drained and coarsely chopped
4 ounces (about 40) tiny cornichon pickles, or substitute 4 ounces (about 4 or 5)
kosher baby dill pickles, finely chopped
1 onion, finely chopped
1 bunch flat-leaf parsley, coarsely chopped
Fine sea salt
Freshly ground black pepper
2 pounds monkfish fillet, about 1 inch thick, cut into 24 equal squares
1 1/4 pound lean slab bacon, 1/4 inch thick, cut into 18 equal squares,
about the same size as the pieces of monkfish
1 cup unseasoned bread crumbs
2 tablespoons peanut oil
2 tablespoons unsalted butter

In a small mixing bowl, whisk together the mayonnaise, capers, pickles, onion, and parsley. Add salt and pepper to taste, keeping in mind that the capers are quite salty.

Transfer to a small serving bowl, cover with plastic wrap, and set aside. (You can make the mayonnaise several hours ahead and chill until serving.)

Thread the monkfish and bacon onto 6 skewers, alternating 4 pieces of fish with 3 pieces of bacon on each skewer, beginning and ending with a piece of fish.

Spread the bread crumbs on a large plate. Season the brochettes with a little bit of salt (remember the bacon is salty) and pepper, then roll each brochette in the bread crumbs until well coated; set aside. Combine the oil and butter in a large skillet and warm over medium heat until the butter melts and the mixture is golden and gently bubbling. Place the brochettes in the skillet and sauté for about 2 minutes on each side, until lightly browned. (If you work in two batches, reserve the cooked brochettes in a just-warm oven.) Transfer to warmed plates and serve immediately, accompanied by the caper-cornichon mayonnaise.

volailles et viandes

POULTRY AND MEAT

baked guinea hen with chestnuts and celery-root puree

SERVES 4

For the celery-root puree:
1 celery root, about 1 pound, peeled and coarsely chopped
2 tablespoons fresh lemon juice
1 cup crème fraîche
8 tablespoons unsalted butter
Fine sea salt
Freshly ground black pepper

For the guinea hen:
1 4–4^1/2 pound guinea hen, giblets removed, blotted dry
Fine sea salt
Freshly ground black pepper
^{1}/2 cup peanut oil
1 clove garlic, coarsely chopped
1 sprig thyme
1 small carrot
1 small onion
^{1}/2 cup dry white wine
8 ounces pearl onions, peeled
One 24-ounce jar chestnuts, drained and blotted dry

TO PREPARE THE CELERY ROOT PUREE: In a bowl, toss the celery root with the lemon juice to prevent discoloring. Bring a large pot of water to a boil. Add the celery root and cook until tender, about 30 minutes, then drain. Scrape the celery root into a food processor and puree until smooth. Add the crème fraîche, 8 tablespoons of the butter, and generous pinches of salt and pepper and pulse until blended. Scrape the puree back into the pot, cover, and set aside, or refrigerate until ready to use. The puree can be prepared several hours ahead.

TO MAKE THE GUINEA HEN: Season the bird inside and out with salt and pepper. In a deep casserole large enough to hold the bird, heat 4 tablespoons of the peanut oil over medium heat. Add the guinea hen and brown it on all sides. Transfer the hen to a platter and lightly tent with aluminum foil. Return the casserole to medium heat and add 2 tablespoons of peanut oil, then the garlic, thyme, carrot, and onion, and sauté for 7–8 minutes, until the garlic and vegetables are tender and just slightly browned.

Pour in the wine and about ½ cup water, and deglaze, scraping up any browned bits stuck to the casserole, and simmer for 5 minutes. Strain the liquid through a fine-mesh sieve into a bowl, pressing on the solids to extract as much liquid as possible; discard the solids and wipe out the casserole.

Add the remaining 2 tablespoons peanut oil to the casserole over medium heat. Add the pearl onions and chestnuts and cook until the onions are lightly browned. Pour the guinea hen liquid over the onions and chestnuts, scraping up all the browned bits. Put the guinea hen in the casserole, breast side up, on top of the onions and chestnuts. Cover the casserole and bake in the middle of the oven until the guinea hen is tender and cooked through, about 1 hour. The juices should run clear when the thigh is pierced with a fork. Taste and adjust the seasonings. Bring the casserole to the table and carve the hen there. Serve garnished with the onions, chestnuts, and sauce, and accompanied by the celery puree.

chicken niçoise with lemon confit and olive cream sauce

SERVES 4 TO 6

4 cups sugar
1 pound lemons, washed and halved
2 chickens, about 3 pounds each
Coarsely ground black pepper
1 tablespoon ground ginger
2 bunches parsley, leaves and
tiny stems only
3 bunches cilantro, leaves and
tiny stems only
1 pound onions, finely chopped

2 heads garlic, peeled and
coarsely chopped
1 cup extra-virgin olive oil
Small pinch of saffron threads
4 tablespoons unsalted butter
$1/3$ cup all-purpose flour
1 cup heavy cream
1 pound Picholine green olives, or other
mild green olives, pitted
Fine sea salt

Warm the sugar and 4 cups cold water over low heat, stirring constantly until all the sugar has dissolved. Raise the heat to high and bring to a boil; cook for about 1 minute, without stirring, until the mixture is clear and syrupy. Remove from the heat, place the bottom of the pan in ice water, then set aside to cool to lukewarm. Add the lemons, stir to coat well, place over very low heat, and cook for $1^{1}/_{2}$—2 hours. With a slotted spoon, transfer the confit to a lightly buttered plate and set aside.

Put the chickens in a large casserole and add a generous pinch of pepper, the ginger, parsley, cilantro, onions, garlic, oil, and saffron. Cover with cold water, bring to a boil over high heat, then reduce the heat to medium and cook for 40 minutes. Meanwhile, preheat the oven to 400° F. In a medium skillet, melt the butter over medium heat. Add the flour, stirring briskly to combine into a smooth paste (called a roux). Remove from the heat and set aside to cool slightly.

Transfer the chickens to a roasting pan, and pat dry; set the cooking liquid aside. Roast the chickens in the center of the oven for 15 minutes, then transfer the pan to a wire rack, cover the chickens loosely with aluminum foil, and set aside. Bring the reserved cooking liquid in the casserole to a boil over high heat and cook, stirring frequently, until it is reduced by half. In a slow, steady stream, pour through a strainer into the roux, whisking constantly to blend. Pour the mixture back into the casserole and bring to a boil, whisking constantly, then reduce the heat to medium, add the cream, and cook, stirring frequently, for 10 minutes, or until the sauce is smooth and oily. Add the olives, season to taste with salt and pepper, and remove from the heat. Transfer the chickens to a warmed serving platter and arrange the confit around them. Drizzle with some of the olive sauce, putting the rest in a warmed sauceboat, and serve immediately.

CHEF'S SUGGESTION: This chicken is delicious served with a rice or semolina pilaf with dried fruits like raisins or apricots. To save time, use raw lemon slices instead of lemon confit.

herbed boneless saddle of lamb

SERVES 4

¹/₂ pound pork caul
One 2-pound boneless saddle of lamb fillet, rolled and tied by your butcher
Coarse sea salt
Freshly ground black pepper
¹/₂ bunch chervil, leaves only, coarsely chopped
¹/₂ bunch dill, leaves only, coarsely chopped
¹/₂ bunch tarragon, leaves only, coarsely chopped
¹/₂ bunch chives, coarsely chopped
¹/₂ bunch flat-leaf parsley, leaves only, coarsely chopped

Preheat the oven to 400° F. Spread out the pork caul on a cotton or linen kitchen towel and pat away any excess moisture. Generously season the lamb fillet with the salt and several turns of the pepper mill. Spread the chervil, dill, tarragon, chives, and parsley over the surface of a platter, then roll the lamb back and forth in the herbs to coat well all over. Place the herbed lamb on top of the pork caul. Wrap the caul snugly around the lamb, then place on an 18-by-18-inch square sheet of heavy-duty aluminum foil; wrap the foil snugly around the lamb and seal the top and sides securely.

Heat an ovenproof skillet over medium-high heat, place the aluminum foil packet in the center, and cook for about 10 minutes, rolling the packet back and forth frequently to brown (through the foil) the entire surface evenly. Transfer to the oven and cook for 8 minutes. Remove from the oven and transfer the pan to a wire rack to rest for 15 minutes.

To serve, remove the aluminum foil, carefully reserving the cooking juices. Lift the lamb off the caul and transfer to a carving board; discard the caul. Slice into ¹/₂-inch slices, divide among 4 warmed serving plates, and serve immediately.

CHEF'S SUGGESTION: This is good accompanied by roasted potatoes, or Potato Gratin, page 52.

rack of lamb with niçoise-style gratin of tomato, zucchini, and onion

SERVES 6

For the Niçoise-style gratin:
7 tablespoons olive oil
4 small zucchini, thinly sliced
2 cloves garlic, finely chopped
1 onion, minced
4 tomatoes, thinly sliced
Fine sea salt
Freshly ground black pepper
$^1/2$ cup unseasoned bread crumbs
1 tablespoon finely chopped parsley
1 teaspoon chopped thyme leaves
3 tablespoons unsalted butter, cut into bits

For the rack of lamb:
2 large racks of lamb (about 2$^1/2$ pounds each, 8 ribs each),
Frenched (trimmed) by the butcher
Fine sea salt
Freshly ground black pepper
$^1/2$ cup peanut oil
1 tablespoon crumbled thyme blossoms, or 1 teaspoon chopped thyme leaves
1 tablespoon finely chopped parsley
$^1/2$ carrot
$^1/2$ onion
1 sprig thyme
2 cloves garlic, crushed

MAKE THE NIÇOISE-STYLE GRATIN: Preheat the oven to 350° F. In a large skillet, heat 2 tablespoons of the oil over medium-high heat. Add the zucchini and sauté until they begin to brown, about 3 minutes. Using a slotted spoon or spatula, transfer zucchini to a plate and set aside. Add 3 tablespoons of the oil to the skillet and heat over medium-low heat. Add the garlic and onion and cook, stirring frequently, until they soften and slightly caramelize without browning, about

12 minutes. Spread the onion mixture over the bottom of a medium gratin dish or a baking dish. Arrange the zucchini and tomatoes on top in a single layer, alternating slices of zucchini with slices of tomato, one slice overlapping another. Sprinkle with salt and pepper. Bake in the center of the oven for 10 minutes. Remove from the oven and raise the temperature to broil. Sprinkle on the bread crumbs, then combine the parsley and thyme and sprinkle over the bread crumbs. Dot the top with the butter and broil just until the butter melts and the top browns. Remove from the oven, drizzle with the remaining 2 tablespoons oil, then set aside on a wire rack until ready to serve.

PREPARE THE RACK OF LAMB: Preheat the oven to 475° F. Season the racks of lamb with salt and pepper. Place them in a roasting pan and wrap the ends of the rack with aluminum foil. Drizzle the peanut oil over the racks, then sprinkle with the thyme blossoms and parsley. Place in the center of the oven and roast for 10 minutes. Reduce the oven temperature to 425° F. and roast for another 10 minutes, or until an instant-read thermometer registers 120° F for rare or 130° F for medium. Remove from the oven, transfer the racks to a warmed platter, cover loosely with aluminum foil to keep warm, and set aside.

Place the roasting pan, with its accumulated juices, over medium heat. Add the carrot, onion, sprig of thyme, and garlic and cook, stirring frequently, until the carrot and onion soften but do not brown, about 5 minutes. Remove and discard all but 1 tablespoon of the oil from the pan. Add 1 1/2 cups water, raise the heat to high, bring the water to a boil, and deglaze the pan, scraping up all the browned bits stuck to the pan. Reduce the heat to medium and cook until the liquid is reduced by half. Season to taste, then strain into a warmed sauce boat and set aside until ready to serve.

To serve, slice the racks into individual chops, and arrange 2 or 3 chops on each of 6 warmed serving plates. Serve immediately, accompanied by the gratin and the sauce on the side.

herb-crusted leg of lamb
on white beans

SERVES 6

1 pound Great Northern beans, soaked
   overnight and rinsed
1 onion, studded with 10 whole cloves;
   plus 1 onion, sliced
1 carrot, peeled
1/2 head garlic, cloves separated,
   unpeeled; plus 3 cloves chopped and
   2 whole
1 tablespoon unsalted butter; plus
   2 tablespoons cut into bits
Fine sea salt
Freshly ground black pepper
1 bunch flat-leaf parsley, leaves only,
   chopped
1 leg of lamb, 4–4 1/2 pounds
1 bunch chervil, leaves only
1 bunch anise, leaves only
1 bunch tarragon, leaves only
7 ounces caul fat, rinsed and spread on
   paper towels
1 sprig thyme
2 tablespoons olive oil

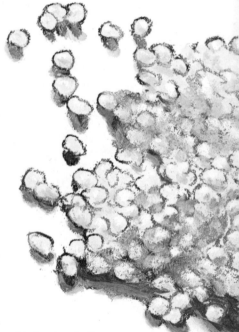

Put the beans in a large casserole. Cover with plenty of water and bring to a boil
over high heat. Skim the surface, add the whole onion, the carrot, and garlic, turn the heat
down to medium-low to maintain a simmer, and cook until the beans are tender, 35 to
40 minutes, or longer if the beans are old. Melt the 1 tablespoon butter in a large, deep casserole
over medium heat. Add the sliced onion and 3 chopped garlic cloves, and gently sauté until the
onion is translucent, about 5 minutes. Stir in the beans, along with a little of their cooking liquid,
and simmer for 3 to 4 minutes. Season to taste with salt and pepper. Sprinkle the parsley over,
cover, and set aside over very low heat until ready to serve.

Meanwhile, preheat the oven to 425° F. Season the lamb with salt and pepper. Sprinkle the chervil, anise, and tarragon over the caul fat. Lay the lamb, fleshy side down, on the herbs. Roll the lamb in the caul fat and tie securely with kitchen string in several places. Place it in a heavy roasting pan along with the remaining 2 cloves garlic and the thyme. Drizzle with the oil, add the remaining 2 tablespoons butter, and cook for 15 minutes on each of its 4 sides, for a total of 1 hour, for medium-rare. Transfer the roast to a platter and let rest.

Pour out excess fat, then place the roasting pan over medium-high heat. Add 2 cups water and deglaze the pan, scraping up any browned bits stuck to the bottom. Bring to a boil over high heat and cook for 5 minutes. Taste and adjust the seasoning. Pour the sauce into a warmed gravy boat. Transfer the beans to a warmed serving platter. Carve the lamb into thick slices, arrange on top of the beans, and serve with the sauce on the side.

CHEF'S SUGGESTION: Cook beans without a cover and without salt: both slow the cooking process.

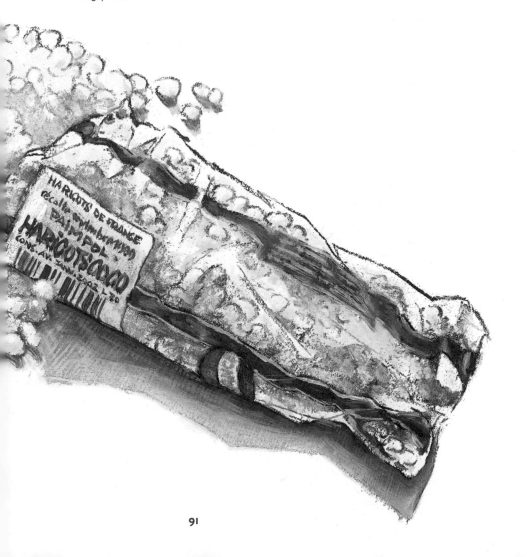

spiced rack of lamb
with honeyed figs

SERVES 4 TO 6

6 tomatoes
7 tablespoons olive oil
1 tablespoon thyme leaves
2 cloves garlic, minced
1 tablespoon cinnamon
1 tablespoon paprika
1 tablespoon ground coriander seeds
2 single racks of lamb (6 ribs each, about
  2 pounds each), Frenched (trimmed)
  by the butcher; reserve the trimmings

Fine sea salt
Freshly ground black pepper
5 tablespoons unsalted butter
6 fresh figs
4 tablespoons acacia or other wildflower
  honey, slightly warmed to syrupy
  consistency

Preheat the oven to 250° F. Arrange the tomatoes in a small baking pan, drizzle with 4 tablespoons of the oil, then sprinkle with the thyme and minced garlic. Bake for 30 minutes. Remove the pan from the oven to a wire rack.

Preheat the oven to 400° F. In a small bowl, blend together the cinnamon, paprika, and coriander. Rub the mixture over the rack of lamb, then drizzle with the remaining 3 tablespoons oil and season with salt and pepper. In a roasting pan, melt 1 tablespoon of the butter over medium-high heat. Sear the racks, turning until light golden brown on all sides. Arrange racks fat side down, transfer to the oven, and roast for 12 minutes; turn over and roast for another 12 minutes, or until an instant-read thermometer registers 120° F for rare, or 130° F for medium. Remove from the oven and transfer the lamb to a platter, cover loosely with aluminum foil to keep warm, and set aside.

Remove and discard all but 1 tablespoon of the fat from the roasting pan and place the pan over medium-high heat. Add the reserved lamb trimmings and cook, stirring frequently, until well browned. Add 2 cups water, bring to a boil, and deglaze the pan. Continue cooking, stirring occasionally, until the liquid is reduced by half. Season to taste with salt and pepper, then strain into a warmed saucepan and keep warm over low heat.

In a medium skillet, melt the remaining butter over medium heat. Add the figs and sauté, turning them occasionally, for 3 minutes. Drizzle the honey over the figs, remove from the heat, and set aside.

Slice the rack into individual chops and divide among 6 warmed serving plates. Garnish each serving with a tomato and a fig, spoon the sauce over the lamb, and serve immediately.

roast saddle of rabbit with mustard, rosemary and fresh pasta

SERVES 6

4 tablespoons olive oil
3 saddles of rabbit, legs attached, 2¹/₂ to 3 pounds total, cut into serving pieces
by your butcher (saddles into 3 equal parts, legs into 2 pieces)
1 carrot, finely diced
1 onion, finely diced
Fine sea salt
Freshly ground black pepper
1 bouquet garni (1 sprig each of parsley and thyme, and 1 bay leaf), tied in cheesecloth
2 tablespoons strong Dijon mustard
1 cup unseasoned bread crumbs
³/₄ cup dry white wine
3 sprigs rosemary, plus 5 or 6 extra for garnish
³/₄ pound fresh thin fettucine
2 tablespoons unsalted butter, melted

Preheat the oven to 300° F. In a large casserole, heat the oil over medium-high heat. Brown the pieces of rabbit to a deep golden color, then add the carrot and onion. Reduce the heat to medium and cook until the onion and carrot have softened but not browned, about 4 minutes. Season generously with salt and pepper, add the bouquet garni, cover, and cook for 5 minutes. Remove from the heat. Spread a thin layer of mustard over each piece of rabbit, sprinkle the bread crumbs over the mustard, pour in the wine, add the 3 sprigs rosemary, and bake in the center of the oven for 10 minutes.

Meanwhile, bring a large pot of salted water to a boil. Add the pasta and cook until just tender; drain well, then toss with the butter and season to taste with salt and pepper. Transfer to a warmed serving bowl. Arrange the rabbit on a warmed serving platter, garnish with sprigs of rosemary, and serve accompanied by the pasta.

roasted veal chops with sautéed vegetables, mushrooms, and herb butter

SERVES 10

1 cup salted butter, softened
3 shallots, finely chopped
2 bunches chives, finely chopped
1 bunch tarragon, finely chopped
1 bunch curly parsley, finely chopped
11 tablespoons unsalted butter
1^1/$_4$ pounds tiny new potatoes, scrubbed
8 carrots, peeled and sliced into ^{1}/$_4$-inch rounds
2 pounds baby fava beans, shelled; or 1 pound frozen baby lima beans
1 pound whole shiitake, oyster, morel, or other seasonal mushrooms; or 1 pound
cremini mushrooms, sliced into ^{1}/$_4$-inch slices
2 cups pearl onions, peeled
1 teaspoon sugar
10 veal chops, about 10 ounces each
Fine sea salt
Freshly ground black pepper
1 cup double-strength veal stock (reduce classic veal stock by half);
or use chicken stock reduced by half

In a small mixing bowl, combine the salted butter with 2 of the shallots, the chives, tarragon, and half the parsley. Mix well with a small wooden spoon to combine. Set aside in the refrigerator.

In a large skillet, melt 4 tablespoons of the unsalted butter over medium heat. Add the potatoes and cook, stirring frequently, until they are tender and cooked through, about 20 minutes. Transfer to a platter and set aside.

Add 2 tablespoons of the butter to the skillet and melt over medium heat. Add the carrots and fava beans and cook, stirring frequently, until the carrots and beans are tender and just slightly golden, about 10 minutes. Transfer to the platter with the potatoes and set aside. Add 2 tablespoons of the butter to the skillet and melt over medium heat. Add the mushrooms and cook, stirring frequently, until the mushrooms wilt slightly and begin to give off their liquid, 7 to 8 minutes. Transfer to the platter with the other vegetables and set aside. Add the remaining 3 tablespoons butter to the skillet and melt over medium heat. Add the onions, stir to coat with the butter, then sprinkle with the sugar and cook, stirring frequently, until the onions are golden brown and lightly caramelized, about 10 minutes. Transfer to the vegetable platter and set aside.

Preheat the oven to 400° F. Season the veal chops with salt and pepper and arrange them in a roasting pan. Roast for a total of 10 to 12 minutes, 5 to 6 minutes on each side for chops cooked medium, but still tender. Meanwhile, in a large casserole, combine the cooked vegetables and the stock and place over medium heat. Simmer for 5 to 6 minutes, until the vegetables are heated through.

Remove the veal from the oven, pour any accumulated juices into the vegetables, and stir to combine; keep the oven at 400° F. Spread the vegetables over the bottom of a large serving platter or large oval copper pan. Arrange the chops over the vegetables, then top each chop with about 1 1/2 tablespoons of the shallot butter.

Place the platter in the oven and heat just long enough for the butter to melt over the chops. Bring to the table and serve immediately.

veal fricassee with basil

SERVES 6

1 shoulder of veal (about 3 pounds), cut into chunks
^{1}/2 cup flour
3 tablespoons olive oil
4 medium onions, minced
2 quarts chicken stock
1 bouquet garni (1 sprig thyme, 1 bay leaf, 1 sprig parsley, 1 small leek,
white and pale green parts only), tied in cheesecloth
1 bunch basil, leaves only
Fine sea salt
Freshly ground black pepper
^{1}/4 cup crème fraîche
Juice of ^{1}/2 lemon

Preheat the oven to 350° F. In a large casserole, combine the veal with just enough cold water to cover. Bring to a boil over high heat, reduce the heat to medium, and simmer for 3 minutes. Remove from the heat, run cold water into the pot to stop the cooking, then drain. Place the flour in a medium mixing bowl, dredge the veal in the flour, and set aside.

In a clean casserole, heat the oil over medium heat, add the onions, stir to coat with oil, and cook 3 to 4 minutes, until the onions soften but do not brown. Add the veal, stir to combine, then place in the center of the oven and bake for 5 minutes, stirring occasionally. Remove from the oven, add the stock, bouquet garni, basil, a generous pinch of salt, and several turns of the pepper mill and stir to combine. Bring to a boil over medium heat, then reduce the heat to medium-low and simmer for about 1^1/2 hours, stirring occasionally.

Using a slotted spoon, transfer the veal to a bowl and set aside. Bring the sauce to a boil over medium-high heat, and cook for 10 minutes at a low boil to reduce the sauce. Add the crème fraîche, reduce heat to medium, and cook for another 5 minutes. Adjust the seasoning, then add the lemon juice and stir to blend. Return the meat to the casserole, stir to cover well with the sauce, then cook for a few minutes, just until heated through. Transfer to a warmed serving dish and serve immediately.

CHEF'S SUGGESTION: Serve this with sautéed baby mushrooms and pearl onions and buttered pasta or rice.

farm-style pork chops with parmesan-chive macaroni

SERVES 6

2 chicken bouillon cubes
1 pound elbow macaroni
3 tablespoons olive oil
6 tablespoons unsalted butter
6 pork chops, about 6 ounces each
Fine sea salt
Freshly ground black pepper
6 teaspoons Dijon mustard
3 cloves garlic, minced; plus 3 whole
  cloves, peeled
1/2 bunch flat-leaf parsley, leaves only,
  finely chopped

6 teaspoons peanut oil
Juice of 1 lemon
1 bunch thyme, leaves only, coarsely
  chopped
1/2 bunch sage, coarsely chopped
1 shallot, minced
1/2 bunch chives, finely chopped
1 cup freshly grated Parmesan cheese

Fill a large pot or a casserole with cold water and bring to a boil over high heat. Add the bouillon cubes and stir to dissolve, then add the macaroni, reduce the heat to medium-high, and cook for 7 minutes. Remove from the heat, cover the pot, and set aside so that the macaroni becomes more tender and plump.

In a large skillet, heat the olive oil and 2 tablespoons of the butter over medium heat.

Season the pork shops lightly with salt and pepper. Add them to the skillet and cook for 5 minutes on each side. Spread 1 side of each chop with 1 teaspoon of the mustard, then remove from the heat. Transfer the chops to a large, warmed plate and sprinkle with the minced garlic and all but 2 tablespoons of the parsley. Drizzle each chop with 1 teaspoon of the peanut oil, then loosely cover the platter with aluminum foil and keep warm in a low oven.

Return the skillet to medium heat, add the lemon juice, and deglaze, scraping up any browned bits stuck to the pan. Add the thyme, whole cloves of garlic, and the sage and stir to combine. Cook for 2 minutes, then remove from the heat, stir in the remaining parsley, and set aside.

Drain the macaroni. In a large, nonstick saucepan, heat the remaining 4 tablespoons butter over medium heat. When melted and frothy, add the macaroni, stir to coat well, and cook, stirring frequently, for 3 minutes. Add the shallot, chives, cheese, and salt and pepper to taste, and stir to combine. Transfer the macaroni to a large, warmed serving platter and arrange the pork chops on top of the macaroni. Remove and discard the whole garlic cloves from the cooking juices, then spoon the juices over the pork chops and macaroni, bring to the table and serve family-style.

ham hocks glazed with caramelized spiced honey, and turnip choucroute

SERVES 4

1¹/₄ cups acacia honey or other wildflower honey
1 whole clove
3 coriander seeds
3 cardamom pods
3 pieces star anise
6 juniper berries
3 tablespoons sherry wine vinegar
3 tablespoons goose or duck fat, or 2 tablespoons unsalted
butter and 1 tablespoon olive oil
1 onion, minced
3 cloves garlic, peeled
1 bay leaf
1 sprig thyme
2 cups dry white wine
2 cups chicken stock
2 pounds turnips, peeled and thinly sliced, cut into ¹/₄-inch-wide strips
Fine sea salt
Freshly ground black pepper
4 ham hocks

In a heavy-bottomed saucepan, combine the honey, clove, coriander seeds, cardamom, star anise, and 3 of the juniper berries, then heat over medium-low heat, stirring occasionally, until the honey is golden. Stir in the vinegar and set aside.

In a large skillet, heat 1 tablespoon of the goose fat over medium-low heat, then add the onion and sauté for 4 to 5 minutes, until tender. Add the garlic, bay leaf, thyme, the remaining juniper berries, and the wine. Bring to a boil and cook until the liquid is reduced by half. Add the stock and simmer for about 15 minutes, or until the liquid is syrupy.

Meanwhile, in a medium skillet, heat the remaining goose fat over medium-low heat. Add the turnips and sauté for 10 minutes, then combine them with the onions. Season to taste with salt and pepper. Cook gently for 5 minutes, then set aside and keep warm until ready to serve.

Meanwhile, preheat the oven to 350° F. Place the ham hocks in a shallow roasting pan, drizzle on the honey mixture, place in the center of the oven, and bake until heated through, basting often with the honey. Divide the turnip choucroute among 4 warmed dinner plates. Place a ham hock on each plate, on top of the turnip choucroute, and serve.

grilled rib steaks with shallots and parsley and bibb lettuce salad

SERVES 4

For the steaks:
2 rib steaks from a standing rib roast, about 1 1/3 pounds each
with the bone, cut 1 3/4 inches thick
Fleur de sel or coarse sea salt
Freshly ground black pepper
4 shallots, finely chopped
1/2 bunch flat-leaf parsley, finely chopped
1/2 cup peanut oil

For the salad:
2 tablespoons sherry vinegar
5 tablespoons extra-virgin olive oil
4 heads Bibb lettuce, left whole or halved;
or 2 heads Boston lettuce, quartered

COOK THE STEAKS: Generously season the steaks with salt and pepper. Heat a heavy, nonstick skillet over medium heat until hot. Place the steaks in the skillet and cook until seared and well crusted on one side, 4–5 minutes. Turn and cook for 4–5 minutes on the other side. Remove from the heat and spoon out excess fat from the pan. Sprinkle the shallots and parsley over the steaks and pat gently into the meat. Drizzle with the peanut oil, tent loosely with aluminum foil, then set aside (unheated) to rest.

MEANWHILE, PREPARE THE VINAIGRETTE: In a small bowl, combine the vinegar with a generous pinch of salt and several turns of the pepper mill and whisk to dissolve the salt. Add the olive oil and whisk to emulsify. Pour over the Bibb lettuce and toss well to coat; set aside.

Transfer the steaks to a cutting board and cut away the bones; place the skillet over low heat. Slice the steak across the grain into 1/3-inch strips and divide among 4 warmed serving plates. Raise the heat under the skillet to medium-high, then pour the carving juices into the skillet and stir with a wooden spoon to combine. Heat for a few seconds, then spoon the juices over each serving. Serve immediately, accompanied by the salad.

plats uniques

ONE-DISH MEALS

salt pork with lentils

SERVES 6

Begin preparations for this recipe about 4^1/2 hours before serving.

3^1/2 pounds meaty salt pork, cut into several large pieces
2 whole cloves
2 medium onions, 1 whole, 1 quartered
1 large carrot, peeled and cut into ^{1}/2-inch slices
1 bouquet garni (1 sprig thyme, 1 bay leaf, 1 sprig parsley), tied in cheesecloth
1 pound (about 2^1/2 cups) imported French green lentils, picked over and well rinsed
Freshly ground black pepper
Fine sea salt
^{1}/4 cup finely chopped parsley

Place the salt pork in a large saucepan, cover with cold water, and set aside to desalt for about 2 hours. Drain, then place the salt pork in a small stockpot, cover it with 2 inches of cold water, and bring to a boil over high heat. Reduce the heat to medium-low, so that water remains at a low boil, and cook for 2 hours, skimming the top frequently. Set aside.

Meanwhile, press the cloves into the 2 ends of the whole onion. In a medium pot, combine the onions with the carrot, bouquet garni, and lentils, cover with cold water by about 1 inch, and bring to a boil over medium heat. Reduce the heat to medium-low, cover, and cook at a simmer for 30 to 35 minutes, until the lentils are tender but still intact. Drain the lentils of any excess liquid, remove and discard the bouquet garni and the onions, and season to taste with several turns of the pepper mill. (Since the salt pork will add salt to the lentils, season with salt only at the end of cooking, if needed.) Set aside.

Drain the salt pork, reserving ^{2}/3 cup of the cooking liquid. Slice the salt pork into 2-inch cubes. In a large, heavy-bottomed casserole, combine the lentils, salt pork, and the reserved cooking liquid, and stir to combine. Bring to a simmer over medium heat and cook for 20 minutes, stirring occasionally. Remove from the heat, season to taste with pepper and salt if necessary, and sprinkle the parsley over. Bring to the table and serve family-style.

grandma's red-wine daube of beef

SERVES 6

Begin preparations for this recipe
one day before serving.

3 bottles (750 ml each) dry red wine
3 pounds beef round (or use a combination
   of round and chuck), cut into large cubes
2 tablespoons flour
$^3/_4$ cup olive oil
3 pounds carrots, cut into $^1/_2$-inch rounds
12 ounces pork rind, blanched 2 minutes in
   boiling water, diced
One slice (about $^1/_8$ pound) country ham,
   finely chopped
$^1/_2$ pound shallots, chopped
Fine sea salt
Freshly ground black pepper
5 teaspoons sugar
$^3/_4$ cup Armagnac or cognac

In a large soup pot or casserole, bring the wine to a boil over medium-high heat. Reduce the heat to low and simmer for 1 hour to reduce and intensify the wine. Set aside.

Dredge the beef in the flour. In a large skillet, heat $^1/_4$ cup of the oil, then add the beef, turning to brown all sides, working in batches if necessary. Transfer the beef to a plate and set aside. In a clean skillet, heat $^1/_4$ cup of the oil over medium-high heat, then add the carrots and sauté for 4 to 5 minutes, until they begin to very lightly brown. Add the pork rind, stir to combine, then stir in the ham and the shallots. Sauté for about 4 minutes, until the shallots soften and begin to turn translucent, but do not brown. Remove from the heat and set aside.

In a large (about 5-quart) casserole, layer the beef and the carrot mixture. Pour in the reduced wine, add about 1 teaspoon salt, 6 or 7 generous turns of the pepper mill, and the sugar. Bring to a boil over medium-high heat, then reduce the heat to low and cook, covered, for 2 to 3 hours, until the beef is very tender and shreds at the touch of a fork. Add the Armagnac, stir to incorporate, then remove from the heat and set aside to cool. Refrigerate overnight.

One hour before serving, reheat the daube, simmering over medium-low heat for 1 hour, and stirring occasionally to prevent sticking. Divide among 6 large, warmed soup plates, and serve.

hachis parmentier:
french shepherd's pie

Begin preparations for this recipe about 4 hours before serving.

1½ pounds beef rump roast, cut into large cubes
2 medium onions
2 young leeks, well washed, halved
2 carrots, peeled and halved
1 bouquet garni (1 sprig thyme, 1 bay leaf, 1 sprig parsley), tied in cheesecloth
Fine sea salt
Freshly ground black pepper
3 cups beef stock

1½ pounds small russet potatoes, peeled and quartered
2 tablespoons unsalted butter
¼ cup milk, warmed
1 tablespoon olive oil
1 onion, finely chopped
1 bunch parsley, leaves only, finely chopped
½ cup beef bouillon
About ¼ cup unseasoned bread crumbs

In a large casserole, combine the beef, 2 whole onions, the leeks, carrots, bouquet garni, a pinch each of salt and pepper, the beef stock, and enough water to cover by 2 inches; stir to combine. Bring to a boil over high heat, then cover, reduce the heat to medium-low, and simmer for 2 to 3 hours, until the beef shreds at the touch of a fork. Add more water if needed. Remove from the heat and set aside to cool. When the meat is cool enough to handle, shred it into a bowl and set aside.

Meanwhile, in a large saucepan, combine the potatoes with enough water to cover and a generous pinch of salt. Bring to a boil over high heat, then reduce the heat to medium and cook for about 30 minutes, until the potatoes are tender when pierced with a fork. Transfer the potatoes to a mixing bowl, add the butter and milk, and, using a potato ricer, a masher or a hand-held electric beater, puree until the mixture is satiny, smooth, and lump-free; set aside.

Preheat the oven to 350° F. In a small skillet, heat the olive oil over medium heat. Add the chopped onion and sauté, stirring frequently, for about 4 minutes, until the onion is soft but not browned; remove from the heat.

In a large mixing bowl, combine the shredded beef, sautéed onion, parsley, and salt and pepper to taste; stir to combine. Transfer the mixture to a baking pan, pour the bouillon over, and braise in the center of the oven for 25 minutes. Remove from the oven and raise the temperature to 400° F. Butter the bottom of a medium baking dish. Spread one-third of the potato puree on the bottom of the dish. Top with half of the beef mixture, then another third of the potato puree, then the other half of the beef mixture, then the remaining potato puree. Sprinkle the bread crumbs evenly over the surface of the potatoes and bake in the center of the oven for 7 to 8 minutes, until the top is lightly browned. Serve immediately.

stewed stuffed capon

ı capon, about 4^1/2 pounds, with giblets
^{3}/4 cup milk
8 cups coarse fresh bread crumbs
7 ounces ham, diced
8 cloves garlic, 3 chopped, 5 whole
3 shallots, chopped
ı tablespoon chopped flat-leaf parsley
ı tablespoon chopped tarragon leaves
Fine sea salt
Freshly ground black pepper
Pinch grated nutmeg
2 eggs, beaten
6 carrots, peeled and cut into 3-inch lengths
5 leeks, well washed, white and light green parts only, cut into 3-inch lengths
3 turnips, peeled and cut into ^{1}/2-inch slices
ı stalk celery, cut into 3-inch lengths
ı onion, studded with ı clove
ı bouquet garni (ı sprig thyme, ı bay leaf, ı sprig parsley, ı small leek,
white and pale green parts only), tied in cheesecloth

Pull off any excess fat from the capon and giblets and discard it along with the gizzard. Finely chop the capon liver and heart. Pour the milk into a large bowl. Add the bread crumbs and let them absorb the milk. Add the ham, the chopped garlic, the shallots, parsley, and tarragon and toss lightly to combine. Season the mixture with salt, pepper, and nutmeg. Stir in the eggs just to blend. Season the capon cavity generously with salt and pepper, then stuff with the bread crumb mixture, taking care not to pack too tightly since the stuffing expands while cooking, and truss closed.

Fill a large, deep stock pot about two-thirds full of water and bring to a boil. Add the capon and simmer gently for 2 hours. Add the vegetables, bouquet garni, and the whole garlic cloves, and cook for 2 more hours. Remove the capon from the broth and tent it with foil to keep warm.

Using a slotted spoon, remove and discard the bouquet garni, garlic, and onion. Divide the vegetables and the stuffing among 6 large warmed soup plates. Cut the legs from the capon. Remove the skin, shred the meat, and divide it among the plates. With a sharp knife, remove the breast in two pieces. Pull the skin off, cut the meat into generous slices on the bias, and lay them over the dark meat. Bring the broth to a boil. Adjust the seasonings to taste, then ladle the hot broth into each plate and serve.

cassoulet

SERVES 6

8 ounces smoked bacon
8 ounces pork rind or fatback
8 ounces garlic sausage
1 onion, studded with 1 clove
2 carrots
1 pound white beans, soaked overnight and rinsed
1 tablespoon vegetable oil
1 small shoulder of lamb, boned, excess fat removed,
cut into 1½-inch cubes, blotted dry
2 tablespoons tomato paste
Fine sea salt
Freshly ground black pepper
7 ounces goose or duck fat
1 pound 6 ounces fresh pork sausage links
1 pound 6 ounces pork loin roast
3 duck legs confit (see Guide to Specialty Stores, page 142)
1 large onion, sliced
6 cloves garlic, finely chopped
2 pounds canned crushed tomatoes
1 sprig fresh thyme or 1 teaspoon dried thyme
½ bunch flat-leaf parsley, leaves only, finely chopped
¾ cup unseasoned bread crumbs

Tie the bacon, pork rind, garlic sausage, clove-studded onion, and carrots together in a large, double layer of cheesecloth, and put with the beans in a large, deep, heavy-bottom casserole. Cover with water at least 3 inches above the top of the beans. Bring to a boil, then turn the heat down and simmer until the beans are almost tender, about 1½ hours. Drain, reserving the cooking liquid. Transfer the beans, bacon, pork rind, and garlic sausage to a bowl, discarding the onion and carrots; cover loosely with foil and set aside.

Meanwhile, in a large casserole, heat the oil over medium-high heat, add the lamb, and brown on all sides. Add 1 tablespoon of the tomato paste and stir to coat. Season with salt and pepper, add about ¾ cup water, cover, and cook over medium heat until tender. In a skillet, heat 1 tablespoon of the goose fat. Add the sausage links and cook over medium heat until brown on all sides and no longer pink in the center. Keep warm.

Preheat the oven to 350° F. Roast the pork loin in a shallow roasting pan for 45 minutes, then remove and cut into $^1/_4$-inch slices. Tent with foil and keep warm. Gently heat the duck confit in a skillet over medium heat. Remove the bones, chop the meat into large pieces, and keep warm.

Turn the oven down to 250° F. Remove the pork rind from the beans and cut into thin strips. Slice the smoked bacon and garlic sausage and set aside. In a large casserole, heat 3 tablespoons of the goose fat over medium-high heat. Add the sliced onions, the garlic, and pork rind and cook gently over medium-low heat until the onions are translucent and golden. Add the tomatoes, the remaining 1 tablespoon tomato paste, the thyme, and the cooked beans. Stir in the cooking liquid from the lamb and about $^1/_2$ cup of the bean cooking liquid, transfer to the oven, and bake for $^1/_2$ hour. Remove from the oven and stir in the parsley.

TO SERVE THE CASSOULET: Heat the oven to 425° F. Spoon the bean mixture into a large, deep ovenproof serving platter or casserole. Add the lamb cubes, bacon, garlic sausage, duck confit, and sausage links, and stir to combine. Sprinkle the bread crumbs over the top, drizzle on the remaining goose fat, and cook until the crumbs are nicely browned. Serve very hot.

navarin of lamb with potatoes

SERVES 6

4 tablespoons olive oil
2 pounds boneless lamb shoulder, cut into 1¹/2-inch cubes
¹/2 pound onions (2 small or 1 large), finely diced
¹/2 pound carrots (about 3 medium), peeled and finely chopped
2 tablespoons flour
1 tablespoon tomato paste
1 bouquet garni (1 sprig thyme, 1 bay leaf, 1 sprig parsley, 1 small leek, white and pale
green parts only), tied in cheesecloth
4 cloves garlic, crushed
Fine sea salt
Freshly ground black pepper
2 pounds tiny new or Yukon Gold potatoes, peeled
¹/2 pound pearl onions, blanched for 1 minute and peeled
1 tablespoon unsalted butter
1 teaspoon sugar
¹/2 bunch curly parsley

Preheat the oven to 350° F. In a heavy-bottom casserole, heat the oil over high heat. Add the lamb and brown quickly on all sides. Add the chopped onions and carrots and stir to combine. Reduce the heat to medium and cook, stirring frequently, until onions soften and begin to look translucent, about 4 minutes. Remove from the heat. Sprinkle the flour over the meat, then place the skillet in the center of the oven and cook until the flour begins to brown, about 12 minutes.

Remove from the oven, add the tomato paste, and stir in with a slotted spoon. Raise the oven temperature to 400° F. Add almost (but not quite) enough room-temperature water to cover the lamb and stir to combine. Over high heat, bring the mixture to a boil. Add the bouquet garni and garlic, season with about 1 teaspoon salt, or to taste, and several turns of the pepper mill, and stir to combine. Cover the casserole and bake in the oven for 40 minutes.

Meanwhile, bring a large pot of water to a boil. Add the potatoes and cook for 2 minutes, then drain and set aside. In a medium saucepan, combine the pearl onions, butter, sugar, and a pinch

of salt with enough water to half-cover the onions. Bring to a
boil over high heat, then reduce the heat and simmer, stirring occasionally, until all the water has evaporated and the onions are slightly
caramelized and tender when pierced with the tip of a knife. Set aside.

Remove the casserole from the oven and discard the bouquet garni. Add the potatoes and stir to
combine. Cover, return to the oven, and cook for about 15 minutes, until the potatoes are tender
when pierced with the tip of a knife. Meanwhile, reheat the pearl onions. Remove the casserole
from the oven, gently stir in the pearl onions and the parsley, and serve immediately.

roast turkey with truffle, chestnut, and chipolata sausage stuffing

SERVES 6

¹/2 pound chipolata sausages, or other moderately spicy sausages, coarsely chopped
¹/2 pound canned whole chestnuts in water, drained and coarsely chopped
One 8- to 10-pound turkey
Fine sea salt
Freshly ground black pepper
2 ounces truffles, finely chopped (see Chef's Suggestion)
¹/2 pound ground pork
¹/4 cup cognac
2 tablespoons unsalted butter
2 tablespoons peanut oil

Preheat the oven to 350° F. Heat a large skillet over medium heat. Add the sausages and cook, stirring frequently, until the sausage just begins to brown. Add the chestnuts and cook, stirring frequently, until the sausage is browned and the chestnuts are lightly browned. Remove from the heat and set aside.

Season the turkey's cavity with salt and pepper. When the sausage-chestnut mixture is cool enough to handle, stuff the turkey's cavity with it and set aside.

In a mixing bowl, combine the truffles, pork, and cognac and mix well. Loosen the skin around the turkey's breast and thighs, then, using your fingertips, gently slide the truffle mixture into the small pockets between the skin and the meat. Stitch the cavity closed with poultry twine, truss the turkey, and place it in the center of a roasting pan surrounded by the turkey neck, liver, and kidneys. Using your hands, spread the butter and oil over the turkey's skin, season well with salt and pepper, and roast for 1¹/2 hours. Cover the turkey lightly with a sheet of aluminum foil to prevent the skin from burning and continue to roast for about another 1¹/2 hours, until the juices run clear when the thigh is pierced with a fork. Remove from the oven and transfer the turkey to a serving platter.

Remove and discard the fat from the roasting pan, then heat the pan over medium-high heat. Add 2¼ cups water and deglaze the pan, scraping up any browned bits stuck to the pan. Season with salt and pepper to taste, reduce the heat to low, and simmer for 4 to 5 minutes. Strain the sauce into a warmed gravy boat. Transfer the sausage stuffing to the center of a warmed serving platter. Slice the turkey and arrange around the stuffing. Serve immediately, accompanied by the sauce.

CHEF'S SUGGESTION: If truffles are not available, substitute 1 cup chopped wild mushrooms, briefly sautéed in 2 tablespoons olive oil and then combined with 2 tablespoons minced parsley.

herb-roasted chicken
à la grand-mère

SERVES 4

For the herb butter:
1 stick (8 tablespoons) unsalted butter, softened
$^1/_4$ bunch each: tarragon, chives, chervil, parsley
2 shallots, finely chopped
Fine sea salt
Freshly ground black pepper

For the chicken:
One 3$^1/_2$- to 4-pound roasting chicken, free-range if possible
3 cloves garlic
2 sprigs fresh thyme
1 bay leaf
2 tablespoons unsalted butter, softened
2 tablespoons peanut oil
Fine sea salt
Freshly ground black pepper
$^1/_2$ carrot, finely diced
$^1/_2$ onion, finely diced
$^1/_4$ cup white wine
Fleur de sel, or coarse sea salt
$^1/_4$ teaspoon crushed black peppercorns

PREPARE THE HERB BUTTER: In a small mixing bowl, combine the butter with the tarragon, chives, chervil, parsley, shallots, and salt and pepper to taste; set aside.

PREPARE THE CHICKEN: Using your fingers, loosen the skin at the neck of the chicken, creating pockets between the skin and the meat over the breasts and around the wings. With your fingers, slide portions of the herb butter into the pockets, pressing the butter into the meat. Place the chicken in a roasting pan, and surround it with the garlic, thyme, and bay leaf. Spread the skin with the butter, drizzle with the oil, then season with salt and pepper. Roast in the center of the oven, turning the pan and basting occasionally, for 25 minutes, then reduce the heat to 375° F and continue roasting, turning the pan, and basting, for about 50 minutes more, until the chicken is deep golden brown, and the juices run clear when the thigh is pierced with a fork. Transfer the chicken to a platter and cover loosely with aluminum foil.

Spoon out and discard the excess fat from the roasting pan, leaving about 1 tablespoon, then add the carrots and onions and cook over medium heat, stirring frequently. Sauté for 4 to 5 minutes, until the onions begin to soften and become translucent. Add the wine and deglaze the pan, scraping up any browned bits stuck to the pan. Add $2/3$ cup water, a pinch of fleur de sel, and the crushed peppercorns, and stir to combine. Raise the heat to high and bring to a boil, then lower the heat to medium and cook, stirring frequently, until the liquid is reduced by one-third. Remove the sauce from the heat and set aside.

Carve and slice the chicken, divide the pieces among 4 warmed serving dishes, spoon the sauce over the chicken, and serve immediately. Or, carve the chicken at the table and serve the sauce on the side.

desserts

DESSERTS

lemon meringue tart

SERVES 6

For the rich, flaky pastry crust:
1³/₄ cups flour
³/₄ cup confectioners' sugar
4 egg yolks
7 tablespoons unsalted butter, cut into bits, softened

For the glazed lemon:
³/₄ cup confectioners' sugar
Peel of 1 lemon, very finely julienned

For the lemon filling:
1³/₄ cups fresh lemon juice
Zest of 2 lemons
2¹/₂ cups granulated sugar
1 cup unsalted butter
6 egg yolks

For the meringue:
3 egg whites
¹/₄ cup granulated sugar

PREPARE THE RICH, FLAKY PASTRY CRUST: Sift the flour and confectioners' sugar into a mixing bowl. Add the egg yolks and the butter and stir well with a wooden spoon to blend; you can continue to blend using your hands and gently kneading the dough. Work the dough until it is soft, smooth, and satiny. It should not be sticky; if it is, add a tablespoon or two of flour and knead until the consistency is right. Remove from the bowl, press into a flat disk, cover with plastic wrap, and refrigerate for about 20 minutes. On a well-floured work surface, using a floured rolling pin, roll out the dough to a circle about 12 inches in diameter. Press into a buttered 10- or 10¹/₂-inch tart pan, ideally one with a removable bottom. Prick the bottom all over with a fork. Trim the excess at the rim to ¹/₂ inch, double over the dough to create a ¹/₄-inch border above the rim, then flute or crimp the edges. Preheat the oven to 400° F. Line the tart shell with aluminum foil and fill with baking weights or dried beans. Bake for 8 minutes. Remove the weights and the aluminum foil and bake for another 8 to 10 minutes, until the shell is dry and just golden. Set the pan aside on a wire rack to cool.

PREPARE THE GLAZED LEMON: In a small saucepan combine the confectioners' sugar and $^3/_4$ cup water, and stir to dissolve the sugar. Add the lemon peel and bring to a boil over medium-high heat. Reduce the heat to low and cook until most of the water has evaporated. Remove from the heat, then transfer the peel to a plate to cool and dry; set aside.

PREPARE THE LEMON FILLING: In a medium saucepan, combine the lemon juice, lemon zest, $1^3/_4$ cups of the sugar, and the butter and bring to a boil over medium-high heat. Meanwhile, in a mixing bowl, combine the egg yolks and the remaining $^3/_4$ cup sugar and whisk briskly until the mixture turns a pale yellow. Add to the lemon mixture and stir to incorporate. Continue cooking for another 5 minutes, or until the mixture is smooth and thickened. Remove from the heat and set aside to cool.

PREPARE THE MERINGUE: In the bowl of an electric mixer, beat the egg whites until soft peaks form. Add the sugar and continue beating until stiff peaks form. Set aside, or refrigerate until ready to use.

ASSEMBLE THE TART: Preheat the oven to 425° F. When all the components have cooled, pour the lemon filling into the tart shell and spread it evenly. Arrange the lemon peel over the top, then top the tart with the meringue, piping it on decoratively or spreading it on with a spatula. Bake for 5 minutes, just until the meringue is firm and dry. Set aside in a cool corner of the kitchen, but not refrigerated, to set for at least 2 hours before serving. This tart is most delicious served within a few hours of baking.

fromage blanc tart

SERVES 6

For the pastry crust:
1 cup flour
7 tablespoons unsalted butter
1/4 teaspoon fine sea salt
1/4 teaspoon sugar
1 egg yolk
1 tablespoon milk

For the filling:
2 cups fromage blanc, drained of excess moisture
1/3 cup superfine sugar
Scant 1/2 cup flour
1/4 cup crème fraîche
2 eggs, beaten

PREPARE THE PASTRY CRUST: In the bowl of a food processor, combine the flour, butter, salt, and sugar. Process for about 10 seconds, until the mixture resembles coarse sand. Add the egg yolk and the milk and pulse 6 to 8 times, just until the dough starts to come together in a ball. (If the dough is too dry, add another tablespoon of milk and pulse a few more times; if the dough is too sticky, add another tablespoon or two of flour and pulse a few more times.) Remove from the bowl, knead in your hands for 2 to 3 minutes, press into a flat disk, cover with plastic wrap, and refrigerate for 30 minutes. Roll out very thin into a circle about 13 inches in diameter. Press into a buttered 10- or 10 1/2-inch tart pan, ideally one with a removable bottom. Prick the bottom all over with a fork. Trim the excess at the rim to 1/2 inch, double over the dough to create a 1/4-inch border above the rim, then flute or crimp the edges. Refrigerate until ready to fill.

Preheat the oven to 350° F.

PREPARE THE FILLING: In a mixing bowl, combine the fromage blanc, sugar, flour, crème fraîche, and eggs and whisk well to blend. Pour the filling into the prepared tart crust and bake in the center of the oven for about 45 minutes, until the filling has set. Transfer to a wire rack to cool. If you're using a pan with a removable bottom, unmold the tart before serving. Serve at room temperature.

raspberries with mascarpone cream and honey-lime sauce

SERVES 6

2 tablespoons liquid honey
Juice of 3 limes
$^1/_2$ cup heavy cream
2 tablespoons confectioners' sugar
1 cup mascarpone cheese
3 pints fresh raspberries

In a small saucepan, warm the honey over low heat. Add the lime juice and stir to blend. Transfer to a small bowl, cover, and refrigerate.

Combine the cream and confectioners' sugar in a medium mixing bowl and whisk or beat with an electric beater until the mixture forms firm, but not stiff, peaks. Place the mascarpone in a medium mixing bowl and gently fold in the whipped cream, adding about one-third at a time, until thoroughly combined but still airy.

Divide the mascarpone cream among the bottoms of 6 individual serving bowls. Top neatly with the raspberries, drizzle with the honey-lime sauce, and serve immediately.

CHEF'S SUGGESTION: You can prepare the mascarpone cream and the honey-lime sauce an hour or two ahead of serving.

sautéed cherries with vanilla ice cream

SERVES 6

11 tablespoons unsalted butter
2 pounds dark red cherries, stoned
6 tablespoons strawberry, raspberry, or red-currant jelly
1½ pints rich vanilla ice cream

In a large skillet, melt the butter over medium-high heat. When the butter just starts to brown lightly, add the cherries, stir to coat them with butter, and sauté for 7 to 8 minutes, until the cherries begin to soften. Add the jelly and 1½ cups water, stir to combine, then cook until the mixture comes to a boil. Remove from the heat, let cool slightly, then transfer to a ceramic bowl. Place a generous scoop of vanilla ice cream in the center of each of six dessert bowls or soup dishes. Spoon the warm cherry mixture on top and serve immediately.

CHEF'S SUGGESTION: The essence of this recipe is the contrast between cold and hot, so it is important not to let the cherries cool too much before serving.

baked spiced pears with pistachio ice cream and chocolate sauce

SERVES 6

For the baked pears:
6 well-shaped Anjou or other pears, just barely ripe, peeled
1 vanilla bean
1 whole clove
12 shelled walnuts
12 shelled pistachio nuts
Four $^1/_4$-inch lemon slices
2 tablespoons salted butter
2 tablespoons sugar
8 ounces prepared puff pastry, cut into $1^1/_2$-inch strips

For the chocolate sauce:
8 ounces semisweet chocolate
8 tablespoons unsalted butter

1 pint pistachio ice cream

PREPARE THE BAKED PEARS: Preheat the oven to 425° F. In a small casserole, arrange the pears in an upright position; if they can't remain upright, trim the bottom slightly to create a flat surface. Add the vanilla bean, clove, walnuts, pistachio nuts, lemon slices, butter, $^3/_4$ cup water, and the sugar. Cover the casserole, then seal the edges with the strips of puff pastry, pressing firmly all around. Bake for 40 minutes. Transfer the casserole to a wire rack to cool.

PREPARE THE CHOCOLATE SAUCE: Melt the chocolate in the top of a double boiler over simmering water. Add the butter and $^1/_3$ cup plus 2 tablespoons water and stir well to blend. When the mixture is hot, remove from the heat and keep warm.

To serve, carefully break the puff pastry seal, keeping the pieces as large as possible. Place a pear in the center of each of 6 dessert plates, and drizzle the cooking juices over them. Place a scoop of ice cream next to each pear, then decorate the plates with the walnuts and pistachio nuts. Place a piece of puff pastry in the center of each scoop of ice cream and serve immediately, accompanied by the chocolate sauce, served in a warmed sauceboat.

bread pudding with candied fruits

SERVES 4

¹/3 cup raisins
¹/2 pound stale white bread, crusts removed, cut into 2-inch cubes (or fresh bread,
cubed and dried in the oven at 175° F for about 1 hour)
1 cup milk
1 egg, beaten
4 tablespoons unsalted butter, melted
6 tablespoons light brown or white sugar
1 teaspoon ground cinnamon
¹/2 teaspoon ground nutmeg
¹/2 teaspoon ground cloves
Zest from ¹/2 lemon
Zest from ¹/2 orange
1 tablespoon crème fraîche, or heavy cream
¹/3 cup mixed candied fruit or candied cherries

Preheat the oven to 325° F. In a small bowl, combine the raisins with 1 cup hot water, and set aside
to plump. In a large mixing bowl, combine the bread and the milk and set aside for 10 minutes.
Add the egg, butter, sugar, spices, lemon and orange zest, and the crème fraîche to the bread
mixture and stir well with a wooden spoon to combine. Drain the raisins well and add to the bread
mixture, then add the candied fruit and stir to combine. Transfer the mixture to a large, buttered
baking dish or soufflé dish, and bake for 1 hour and 15 minutes, or until the top of the pudding is
golden brown. Remove to a wire rack to cool. Serve slightly warm.

mousse au chocolat

9 ounces semisweet chocolate, coarsely chopped
8 tablespoons unsalted butter, cut into bits
4 large eggs, separated
$^{1}/_{4}$ cup sugar

Melt the chocolate in the top of a double boiler over simmering water. Add the butter bit by bit, stirring well with a wooden spoon to incorporate. Remove from the heat and, one by one, add the egg yolks, stirring to incorporate; set aside.

In the bowl of an electric mixer, combine the egg whites and the sugar and beat until stiff peaks form. Using a spatula, gently fold the egg whites into the chocolate mixture, trying to maintain as much air and volume as possible. Transfer to a serving bowl and refrigerate for at least 2 hours. Spoon into individual dessert bowls and serve.

rich layered chocolate tart

For the rich pastry crust:
3/4 cup unsalted butter, cut into bits and slightly softened
1 cup confectioners' sugar
2 large eggs, beaten
1/2 teaspoon vanilla extract
2 tablespoons ground blanched almonds
1/2 teaspoon fine sea salt
2 cups all-purpose flour

For the chocolate sponge:
5 ounces top-quality bittersweet chocolate
3 tablespoons unsalted butter
3 egg whites, at room temperature
1/3 cup sugar
Scant 1/2 cup flour
4 egg yolks

For the chocolate filling:
8 egg yolks
6 ounces sugar
1 quart heavy cream
1 pound 9 ounces top-quality bittersweet chocolate, coarsely chopped

For the chocolate icing:
7 ounces dark chocolate, coarsely chopped
3 tablespoons unsalted butter, softened

PREPARE THE RICH PASTRY CRUST: In a food processor, combine the butter, confectioners' sugar, eggs, vanilla, almonds, and salt and process until smooth. Add the flour 1/2 cup at a time, pulsing after each addition, until the flour is blended and the dough just comes together. If the dough is sticky, add 2 more tablespoons flour and process until blended. Gather the dough into a ball, then press into a flat disk, cover with plastic wrap, and refrigerate for 1 hour.

Preheat the oven to 375° F. Butter and flour a 9-inch tart pan. On a lightly floured board and using a lightly floured rolling pin, roll the pastry into a circle about 1/8 inch thick and about 11 inches in diameter. Transfer it to the pan, trim the edges so that $1/2$ inch extends above the rim. Fold it over upon itself to create a doubled $1/4$-inch border above the rim. Flute the edges and prick the bottom all over with a fork. Line the tart shell with aluminum foil, and fill with baking weights or dried beans. Bake for 10 minutes to set. Remove the weights and foil, bake for another 7 to 10 minutes, until the crust is pale golden, then transfer the pan to a wire rack and cool.

PREPARE THE CHOCOLATE SPONGE: Preheat the oven to 400° F. Line a 9-inch cake pan with parchment paper. In the top of a double boiler over simmering water, melt the chocolate with the butter, stirring to blend. Set aside to cool slightly. With a whisk, beat the egg whites and sugar until soft peaks form. Gently fold the whites into the chocolate, add the flour and egg yolks, and fold them in. Scrape the mixture into the pan and bake in the middle of the oven for about 15 minutes, or until a toothpick comes out clean when inserted near the center of the cake. Remove and let cool, then invert and unmold. Gently pull off the parchment.

PREPARE THE CHOCOLATE FILLING: In a heavy saucepan, whisk the egg yolks and sugar until they are pale yellow. In a separate saucepan, bring the cream just to a boil, then pour it in a thick stream into the egg yolk mixture, whisking to blend. Place the pan over low heat and cook, stirring continuously, until the cream coats a wooden spoon, about 5 minutes.

Put the chocolate in a bowl. Pour the hot cream mixture in a steady stream over the chocolate, stirring continuously until the mixture is smooth. Let it cool to room temperature. Pour about two-thirds of the filling into the tart shell. Place the sponge cake over it, then add the remaining filling, spreading it with a spatula to cover evenly.

PREPARE THE ICING: Melt the chocolate in the top of a double boiler over simmering water. Remove from the heat, then add the softened butter, stirring to blend. Seat aside to cool until spreadable. Spread the icing evenly over the top and sides of the cake with a metal spatula. Serve at room temperature.

chocolate-raspberry log

SERVES 6

For the chocolate mousse:
10 ounces unsweetened dark chocolate
3 tablespoons unsalted butter
9 egg whites
3/4 cup superfine sugar
7 egg yolks, beaten

For the raspberry sauce:
1 pint (2 cups) fresh raspberries
2/3 cup sugar
1 teaspoon fresh lemon juice

For the cake:
6 eggs, separated
1 1/4 cups superfine sugar
1 cup all-purpose flour
1 1/2 tablespoons cocoa powder
1 tablespoon raspberry liqueur
Raspberry preserves

PREPARE THE CHOCOLATE MOUSSE: In a heavy saucepan or the top of a double boiler, melt the chocolate and butter, and stir to blend. Set aside to cool slightly. Beat the egg whites along with the sugar until stiff but not dry peaks form. Stir the egg yolks into the chocolate mixture, then gently fold in the egg white mixture with a rubber spatula. Set aside.

PREPARE THE RASPBERRY SAUCE: In a heavy-bottom saucepan, combine the raspberries and sugar, bring to a boil, and cook for 2 minutes, breaking up the raspberries with a wooden spoon. Add as much water as necessary to the mixture to make a sauce consistency. Add the lemon juice and boil for 2 more minutes. Strain through a fine-mesh sieve and set aside.

PREPARE THE CAKE: Preheat the oven to 400° F. Line a jelly roll pan with parchment paper. In a large bowl, combine the egg whites and 3/4 cup of the sugar and beat until soft peaks form. In a separate bowl, blend the egg yolks and the flour, then stir in the cocoa powder until evenly mixed. Gently fold in the egg white mixture with a rubber spatula. Spread the batter on the prepared pan and cook in the middle of the oven for 8 minutes. Remove, cover with a clean tea towel, and invert onto a sheet of aluminum foil the same size as the cake. Carefully pull off the parchment paper.

Mix 7 tablespoons water, the remaining $1/2$ cup sugar and the raspberry liqueur together and brush it on the cake to saturate. With a metal spatula, spread a thin layer of raspberry preserves over the cake, then a layer of chocolate mousse. Starting at a long edge, and using the foil to help roll, tightly roll up the cake, ending with the seam at the bottom. Place on a plate. Spread the remaining chocolate mousse over the log, including the ends. Decorate with the tines of a fork to resemble a log, if desired. Cut the cake into serving portions with a serrated knife and serve with a generous spoonful of the raspberry sauce.

crème brûlée

SERVES 6

5 vanilla beans, split lengthwise
1 cup milk
2^3/$_4$ cups heavy cream
9 egg yolks
^{3}/$_4$ cup sugar
^{1}/$_2$ cup dark brown sugar

Preheat the oven to 200° F. Using the tip of a small, sharp knife, scrape the insides of the vanilla beans into the milk. Pour into a medium saucepan, add the cream, and bring to a boil over medium-high heat. Remove from the heat and set aside for 30 to 40 minutes to allow the vanilla to infuse the milk mixture. Line a fine sieve with 3 or 4 layers of cheesecloth, then strain the mixture into a large, clean bowl and set aside.

In a large mixing bowl, combine the egg yolks and the white sugar and mix together well with a wooden spoon. Little by little, add the milk mixture, stirring well with the wooden spoon to blend. Again using a sieve lined with cheesecloth, strain the mixture into a clean bowl. Using a ladle, divide the mixture among 6 shallow, 6-inch round baking dishes, or use 5- or 6-inch ramekins, or even oven-proof 6-inch soup dishes. Place them in the center of the oven and bake for about 2 hours, until the center of the crème brûlées are just set and no longer tremble when you gently shake them. Transfer the dishes to a wire rack to cool to room temperature, then refrigerate for at least 3 hours.

Just before serving, preheat the broiler. Using a paper towel, gently dry the tops of the crème brûlées of any accumulated moisture, then, using a small sieve, sprinkle evenly with the brown sugar. Place under the broiler for just a few seconds, just long enough for the sugar to form a firm crust; do not let the sugar burn. Serve immediately.

crêpes filled with grand marnier cream

SERVES 6

For the Grand Marnier cream:
4 egg yolks
1/2 cup sugar
1/3 cup flour
2 cups milk
1/2 vanilla bean, split lengthwise
1/4 cup Grand Marnier

For the crêpes:
2 cups flour
1/2 cup, plus 6 tablespoons sugar
1/2 teaspoon fine sea salt
6 eggs
Zest of 1 lemon
Zest of 1 orange
4 cups milk
4 tablespoons unsalted butter, melted

PREPARE THE GRAND MARNIER CREAM: Combine the egg yolks and sugar, and whisk briskly until the mixture turns pale yellow. Add the flour and blend; set aside. In a saucepan, bring the milk and the vanilla bean to a boil over medium-high heat. Remove from the heat, remove and discard the vanilla bean (or rinse and save for another use), then slowly pour into the egg mixture, while whisking to blend. Return the mixture to the saucepan and bring to a boil over medium-high heat. Reduce the heat to medium-low and cook for 3 to 4 minutes, stirring constantly, until the mixture has thickened. Remove from the heat, stir in the Grand Marnier, spread plastic wrap over the surface of the cream, and set aside to cool to room temperature; refrigerate until ready to use.

PREPARE THE CRÊPES: Combine the flour, 1/2 cup of the sugar, and the salt in a large bowl and form a well in the middle. Add the eggs to the center of the well. Using a whisk, gradually blend the eggs with the flour mixture, incorporating the dry ingredients a little at a time. Add the lemon and orange zest. Add the milk, pouring it in a bit at a time and whisking constantly until the batter is very smooth. Strain the batter through a sieve into a clean bowl, cover with plastic wrap, and set aside for 1 hour.

Shortly before serving, brush a 5- to 6-inch crêpe pan or skillet with melted butter and wipe out any excess. Heat over medium heat until sizzling hot. Spoon in 2 to 3 tablespoons of the batter and swirl the pan to spread the batter over the surface, coating the bottom. Cook the crêpe until light golden brown on the bottom, then flip. Transfer to a heated plate and repeat, buttering the pan as needed to prevent sticking, and stacking the finished crêpes one on top of the other, until you have 18 crêpes. Save any extra batter for another use.

To fill the crêpes, spread 1/4 cup of the filling down the center third of each crêpe, then roll into loose cylinders. Place on a serving plate seam side down. Repeat with the remaining crêpes, arranging 3 crêpes on each plate. Sprinkle each serving with about 1 tablespoon sugar and serve immediately.

galette des rois: epiphany cake

SERVES 6

8 tablespoons unsalted butter, cut into bits, at room temperature
$^1/_2$ cup confectioners' sugar
$^2/_3$ cup almond powder, or 3 ounces slivered almonds, very finely ground
1 teaspoon cornstarch
3 eggs
$^1/_8$ teaspoon almond extract
$1^1/_4$ pounds prepared puff pastry dough, divided in half
1 little charm (optional; see Chef's Suggestion)

In the bowl of an electric mixer, spread and soften the butter, using a rubber spatula. Add the confectioners' sugar, ground almond powder, cornstarch, 2 of the eggs, and the almond extract and mix on low speed until completely blended. Set aside.

On a floured work surface, using a floured rolling pin, roll out each portion of puff pastry into circles $^1/_8$-inch thick and 12 inches in diameter. Transfer both to lightly floured plates and refrigerate for 20 minutes. Using a long metal spatula, spread the butter-almond mixture evenly over one pastry circle, leaving a $^1/_2$-inch border bare. In a small bowl, beat the remaining egg. Using a pastry brush, brush the edge of the filled circle of dough with the egg. Place the second pastry circle on top and press the edges all around to seal. Using the tip of a paring knife, score the top with diagonal $^1/_2$-inch-long incisions about $^1/_2$ inch apart around the border, cutting from the edges toward the center. If you are inserting a charm, insert now, pushing it through one of the incisions a couple inches from the border. Transfer the pastry to a moistened baking sheet. Evenly brush the top with egg. Using the tip of a sharp paring knife, and not cutting completely through the dough, score the top between the border decorations with 10 parallel lines; between these lines score with short diagonal strokes, alternating the direction up or down from one section to the next to create a chevron pattern. Refrigerate for 30 minutes.

Preheat the oven to 450° F. Place the pastry in the center of the oven, lower the heat to 425° F, and bake for about 30 minutes, until the top is puffy and golden brown. Transfer to a wire rack to cool. Serve just warm or at room temperature.

CHEF'S SUGGESTION: This is the classic cake served in France on Twelfth Night—Epiphany. Traditionally, when you buy this cake in a pastry shop, it comes with a golden paper crown. Inside the cake a little plastic or ceramic charm is hidden (watch out when you bite into a slice!), and whoever has the piece with the charm in it is the "king" and gets to wear the crown during dessert.

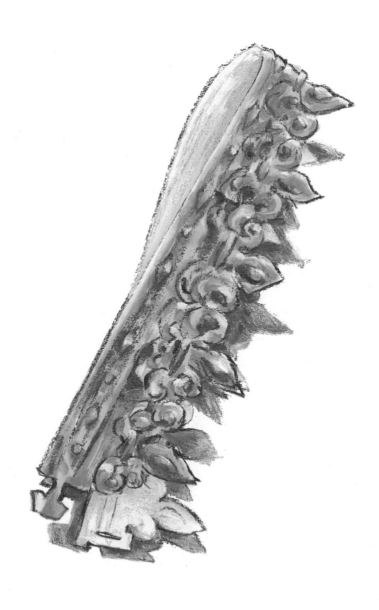

caramelized rice pudding

SERVES 6

1 cup heavy cream
4 cups milk
2 vanilla beans
²/3 cup Arborio rice, well-rinsed in cold running water, drained
³/4 cup sugar

Place the cream in the bowl of an electric mixer, and beat until firm, but not stiff, peaks form. Refrigerate until ready to use.

Preheat the oven to 300° F. Combine the milk and the vanilla beans in a large saucepan. Place over medium-high heat and bring to a boil. Add the rice, stir, then reduce the heat to low and cook, stirring constantly, until the rice is tender, the grains opened, and three-quarters of the liquid has been absorbed, 12 to 15 minutes. Remove from the heat and set aside.

In a small saucepan, combine the sugar with 2¹/2 tablespoons water, place over high heat, and stir to dissolve the sugar. Bring to a boil and cook, without stirring, until the mixture caramelizes, turning a deep golden brown. Remove from the heat, stir, then pour into a medium baking dish. Spoon the rice mixture over the caramel and bake in the center of the oven for 20 minutes. Remove from the oven, then transfer the mixture to a large mixing bowl and set aside to cool to room temperature.

Add the whipped cream and delicately incorporate, mixing carefully with a wooden spoon or a spatula to maintain as much air as possible in the whipped cream. Spoon into serving bowls and serve immediately.

CHEF'S SUGGESTION: Serve plain, or accompanied by a fruit compote or vanilla ice cream.

crunchy dark chocolate "corks"

SERVES 6

1 pound dark chocolate, broken into bits
1/2 pound dark chocolate, finely chopped
2 cups Rice Krispies or other puffed rice cereal

Melt the broken-up chocolate in the top of a double-boiler over simmering water. Take care not to let the chocolate get too hot; remove from the heat as soon as all the chocolate has melted, then add the finely chopped chocolate and stir slowly to blend. Add the Rice Krispies and stir until thoroughly incorporated; set aside to cool slightly.

Lightly butter a large sheet of kitchen parchment and place over a large platter. When the chocolate mixture is lukewarm, form it into cork shapes, using about 2 tablespoons of the mixture per piece. Place each piece on the kitchen parchment. When all the pieces are formed, set the platter in the coolest part of your kitchen to cool. Serve as a dessert or teatime treat.

CHEF'S SUGGESTION: Children love these, and love to help make them, too!

nantes-style rum cake

SERVES 8

Begin preparations for this recipe one day before serving.

For the rum syrup:
^{1}/2 cup sugar
Juice of 1 orange
1 cup dark rum

For the cake:
8 tablespoons unsalted butter, slightly softened
^{1}/2 cup sugar
Zest of 1 orange
3 egg yolks
Fine sea salt
1 teaspoon baking powder
1 cup almond powder, or 4 ounces slivered almonds, very finely ground
3 egg whites, beaten until stiff peaks form
8 whole toasted almonds
^{1}/2 cup apricot jam

PREPARE THE RUM SYRUP: In a saucepan, combine the sugar with ^{1}/3 cup plus 2 tablespoons water and bring to a boil, stirring frequently, over medium-high heat. When all the sugar has dissolved, add the orange juice and the rum and stir to blend. Remove from the heat and set aside to cool.

PREPARE THE CAKE: Preheat the oven to 350° F. Butter a 9-inch removable-bottom tart pan, ideally with smooth rather than fluted sides, or a 9-inch springform cake pan.

In a mixing bowl, combine the butter, sugar, orange zest, and egg yolks and beat with a whisk or an electric beater until the mixture is smoothly blended. Add a pinch of salt, baking powder, and almond powder and mix to combine. Add the egg whites and, using a spatula, gently fold in, maintaining as much volume as possible. Pour the mixture into the prepared tart pan. Bake in the center of the oven for 20 to 30 minutes, until the cake is puffy and golden brown on top. Transfer to a wire rack to cool. While the cake is still slightly warm, unmold it and place back on the wire rack with a large sheet of kitchen parchment underneath. Using a teaspoon, drizzle the rum syrup over the cake. Do a little at a time, allowing the syrup to completely soak in before drizzling more; reserve a little of the syrup. The cake should eventually be well soaked with rum. Place the wire rack, with the cake on top, on a large plate, loosely cover with plastic wrap, and refrigerate for 24 hours.

An hour or so before serving, combine the apricot jam with 3 tablespoons water in a small saucepan and heat over medium heat, stirring frequently, until the jam melts and blends with the water. Strain into a small bowl and set aside to cool to room temperature. Remove the cake from the refrigerator and, if any dry spots are visible, drizzle a little bit of the reserved syrup over them. Arrange the almonds decoratively around the cake, then, using a pastry brush, gently glaze the top and sides with the apricot mixture. Refrigerate for 30 minutes, then serve.

honeyed madeleines

MAKES ABOUT 30

Begin preparations for this recipe one day before serving.

14 tablespoons unsalted butter, plus 2 to 3 tablespoons unsalted butter,
softened, for greasing madeleine molds
3 large eggs
Scant $^3/_4$ cup sugar
2 tablespoons liquid honey
$^1/_2$ cup milk
1 tablespoon vanilla extract
$1^2/_3$ cups flour
$2^1/_2$ teaspoons baking powder

In a small skillet over medium heat, melt the 14 tablespoons butter and cook until very lightly browned, 3 to 4 minutes. Remove from the heat, strain through a sieve into a bowl, and let cool until lukewarm. Meanwhile, in the bowl of an electric mixer, combine the eggs, sugar, honey, milk, and vanilla extract, and beat until well blended. Add the flour and baking powder and beat to incorporate. Add the melted butter and, using the lowest setting on the mixer, or a wooden spoon, delicately mix until blended.

Transfer the batter into a bowl just large enough to hold it, cover with plastic wrap, and refrigerate for 24 hours.

Preheat the oven to 450° F. Using the softened butter and a pastry brush, grease and flour 1 or 2 sheets of madeleine molds, enough to make about 30 madeleines. Spoon or pipe about 1 tablespoon of the batter into each mold, filling each to the rim. Set on a baking sheet and place in the center of the oven. Bake for 6 minutes, then lower the temperature to 400° F. and bake for another 6 minutes, or until the madeleines are golden. Place the molds on a wire rack, unmold the cakes immediately, and transfer to a wire rack to cool. Madeleines are most delicious when served slightly warm from the oven, but they can be stored for up to a week in an airtight container.

recipe index

A

Artichoke Bottoms with Celery Root Puree and Marrow 28–29

Asparagus Fricassee with Soft-Boiled Egg 31

B

Baked Guinea Hen with Chestnuts and Celery-Root Puree 84–85

Baked Spiced Pears with Pistachio Ice Cream and Chocolate Sauce 123

Baked Whitefish in Salt Crust 78–79

Bow-Tie Pasta with Clam Sauce 60

Bread Pudding with Candied Fruits 124

Broccoli and Cauliflower Gratin with Ham 50–51

C

Caramelized Rice Pudding 134

Carpaccio of Marinated Duck Foie Gras 19

Cassoulet 108–109

Celery Root in Parsley-Mustard Mayonnaise 26

Chestnut Soup with Foie Gras, Cabbage, White Beans, and Porcini Mushrooms 10–11

Chicken Niçoise with Lemon Confit and Olive Cream Sauce 86

Chilled Cream of Lima Bean Soup with Rosemary 12–13

Chocolate-Raspberry Log 128–129

Clams with Thyme *en Papillote* 34

Cod Fillets with Chorizo Scales and White Bean Puree 72–73

Cold Lobster with Apple, Avocado, and Vegetable Salad 42–43

Confit of Duck Foie Gras 21

Cream of Lentil Soup Garnished with Bacon, Croutons, and Chives 17

Cream of Pumpkin Soup with Diced Gruyère and Buttered Croutons 14

Crème Brûlée 130

Crêpes Filled with Grand Marnier Cream 131

Crumb-Topped Sea Bass with Sautéed Pears, Lemon Zest, and Baby Spinach Salad 76–77

Crunchy Dark Chocolate "Corks" 135

E

Eggplant Caviar 47

Eggplant Stuffed with Tomato, Basil, Parmesan, and Ham 54–55

Endive Gratin with Ham 49

Essence of Langoustine Soup 15

F

Farm-Style Pork Chops with Parmesan-Chive Macaroni 97

Fried Zucchini Blossoms 48

Fromage Blanc Tart 120

G

Galette des Rois: Epiphany Cake 132–133

Grandma's Red-Wine Daube of Beef 105

Grilled Rib Steaks with Shallots and Parsley and Bibb Lettuce Salad 100–101

H

Hachis Parmentier: French Shepherd's Pie 106

Hake Crusted with Coarse Pepper and Polenta with Olives 71

Ham Hocks Glazed with Caramelized Spiced Honey and Turnip Choucroute 98–99

Hearty Tomato Soup with Vermicelli and Olive Oil Garnish 9

Herb-Crusted Leg of Lamb on White Beans 90–91

Herbed Boneless Saddle of Lamb 87

Herb-Roasted Chicken à la Grand-mère 114–115

Honeyed Madeleines 138–139

L

Lasagna Salad with Sautéed Squid and Parmesan Shavings in Sherry Vinaigrette 62–63

Lemon Meringue Tart 118–119

Lemon-Marinated Fresh Anchovies 32

Lime-Marinated Sea Scallops with Dill 39

M

Mackerel and Horseradish Sauce with Yellow
   Fingerling Potato Salad 38
Mousse au Chocolat 125
Muenster Ravioli 61
Mussels *en Papillote* 33

N

Nantes-Style Rum Cake 136-137
Navarin of Lamb with Potatoes 110-111
Nut-Crusted Baked Salmon with Lamb's Lettuce
   Salad 80

O

Oysters *en Gelée* with Shallot Confit 36-37
Oysters with a *Granité* of Their Juices and Sautéed
   Chipolata Sausage 35

P

Parsleyed Salsify 46
Pasta with Pesto and Shellfish 58-59
Potato Cake Darphin 53
Potato Gratin 52
Provençal Tomato Tart with Tapenade 24-25
Pureed Vegetable and Herb Soup 8

R

Rack of Lamb with Niçoise-Style Gratin of Tomato,
   Zucchini, and Onion 88-89
Raspberries with Mascarpone Cream and
   Honey-Lime Sauce 121
Red Snapper with Harissa and Figs Roasted with
   Sesame Seeds 68-69
Rich Layered Chocolate Tart 126-127
Roast Saddle of Rabbit with Mustard, Rosemary,
   and Fresh Pasta 93
Roast Turkey with Truffle, Chestnut, and Chipolata
   Sausage Stuffing 112-113

Roasted Bay Scallops with Chive Butter 66
Roasted Veal Chops with Sautéed Vegetables,
   Mushrooms, and Herb Butter 94-95

S

Salt Cod, Leek, and Potato Soup with Chorizo
   Garnish 16
Salt-Pork with Lentils 104
Sautéed Cherries with Vanilla Ice Cream 122
Sautéed Duck Foie Gras with Gingerbread Coating
   22-23
Sautéed Fillet of Striped Bass with Sorrel, Capers, and
   Anchovies 74-75
Sautéed Hearts of Baby Artichokes 27
Sautéed Monkfish and Bacon Brochettes with
   Caper-Cornichon Mayonnaise 81
Sautéed Scallops with Endives and Bitter-Orange
   Butter 67
Sea Scallop Salad with Parmesan Shavings and
   Sherry Vinaigrette 40-41
Spiced Rack of Lamb with Honeyed Figs 92
Stewed Stuffed Capon 107
Stuffed Tomatoes with Skate, Shallots, and Herbs 70

T

Tagliatelle with Asparagus and Smoked Salmon
   56-57
Terrine of Duck Foie Gras 18

V

Veal Fricassee with Basil 96
Vegetable Tempura with Soy-Flavored Tartar Sauce
   30

W

Warm Fresh Duck Foie Gras with Caramelized Grapes
   20

guide to specialty stores

For a wide variety of olive oils, nut oils, vinegars, salts, peppers, olives, sugars, vanilla beans, and much more, contact the following companies for information or a catalogue:

BALDUCCI'S
424 Avenue of the Americas
New York, NY 10011
Tel.: 800-822-1444 or
212-673-2600

DEAN & DELUCA
560 Broadway
New York, NY 10012
Tel.: 800-221-7714 or
212-431-1691
www.deananddeluca.com

SWEET CELEBRATIONS INC.
P.O. Box 39426
Edina, MN 55439-0426
Tel.: 800-328-6722 or
612-943-1508
www.sweetc.com

SALUMERIA ITALIANA
151 Richmond Street
Boston, MA 02109-1414
Tel.: 800-400-5916; or
617-523-8743
Fax: 617-523-4946

For a selection of classic French stocks, reductions, and sauces, such as demi-glace, glace de viande, concentrated vegetable and seafood stocks, and rendered duck fat:

MORE THAN GOURMET
Tel.: 800-860-9389
www.morethangourmet.com

For excellent fromage blanc (which freezes well so you could buy in quantity and freeze to amortize shipping costs), crème fraîche, rich, cultured butter and other dairy products:

VERMONT BUTTER AND CHEESE COMPANY
P.O. Box 95
Websterville, VT 05678
Tel.: 800-884-6287 or
802-479-9371
www.vtbutterandcheeseco.com

For a selection of goat cheese —fresh, aged, and herbed:

LITTLE RAINBOW CHÈVRE
15 Doe Hill Road
Hillsdale, NY 12529
Tel.: 518-325-4628
www.littlerainbow.com

For a broad range of domestic and imported cheeses, cut to order before shipping, as well as crème fraîche, and fromage blanc:

IDEAL CHEESE SHOP, LTD.
942 First Avenue
New York, NY 10022
Tel.: 800-382-0109 or
212-688-7579
Fax: 212-223-1245
www.idealcheese.com

For domestic foie gras; fresh ducks, geese, and game; tasty terrines, pâtés, and prepared entrees:

D'ARTAGNAN
152 East 46th Street
New York, NY 10017
Tel.: 800-DARTAGN
212-687-0300

For smoked eastern and western salmon:

DUCKTRAP RIVER FISH FARM
57 Little River Drive
Belfast, ME 04915
Tel.: 207-763-3960
or 800-828-3825
www.ducktrap.com

For succulent Maine sea scallops, Maine lobsters, excellent seasonal fish, and exclusive lines of custom-smoked salmon:

BROWNE TRADING COMPANY
260 Commercial Street
Portland, ME 04101
Tel.: 800-944-7848 or
207-766-2402
Fax: 207-766-2404
www.browne-trading.com

For seasonal French produce, such as wild mushrooms, lamb's lettuce, truffles, truffle juice, and more:

MARCHÉ AUX DÉLICES
New York, NY 10028
Tel.: 888-547-5471
Fax: 413-604-2789
www.auxdelices.com

For truffles, truffle juice, canned foie gras, and caviar:

URBANI TRUFFLES
29-24 40th Avenue
Long Island City, NY 11101
Tel.: 800-281-2330 or
718-392-5050
Fax: 718-392-1704
www.urbani.com

If your travel plans take you to Paris, Christian and Catherine Constant would be delighted to welcome you to Le Violon D'Ingres. Reserve several days in advance.

LE VIOLON D'INGRES
135 rue Saint-Dominique
75007 Paris, France
Tel.: 01-45-55-15-05
Fax.: 01-45-55-48-42
violondingres@wanadoo.fr

Open for dinner
Tuesday-Saturday.

conversion chart

Weight Equivalents

The metric weights given in this chart are not exact equivalents, but have been rounded up or down slightly to make measuring easier.

AVOIRDUPOIS	METRIC
$1/4$ oz	7 g
$1/2$ oz	15 g
1 oz	30 g
2 oz	60 g
3 oz	90 g
4 oz	115 g
5 oz	150 g
6 oz	175 g
7 oz	200 g
8 oz ($1/2$ lb)	225 g
9 oz	250 g
10 oz	300 g
11 oz	325 g
12 oz	350 g
13 oz	375 g
14 oz	400 g
15 oz	425 g
16 oz (1 lb)	450 g
$1/2$ lb	750 g
2 lb	900 g
$2 1/4$ lb	1 kg
3 lb	1.4 kg
4 lb	1.8 kg

Volume Equivalents

These are not exact equivalents for American cups and spoons, but have been rounded up or down slightly to make measuring easier.

AMERICAN	METRIC	IMPERIAL
$1/4$ t	1.2 ml	
$1/2$ t	2.5 ml	
1 t	5.0 ml	
$1/2$ T (1.5 t)	7.5 ml	
1 T (3 t)	15 ml	
$1/4$ cup (4 T)	60 ml	2 fl oz
$1/3$ cup (5 T)	75 ml	$2 1/2$ fl oz
$1/2$ cup (8 T)	125 ml	4 fl oz
$2/3$ cup (10 T)	150 ml	5 fl oz
$3/4$ cup (12 T)	175 ml	6 fl oz
1 cup (16 T)	250 ml	8 fl oz
$1 1/4$ cups	300 ml	10 fl oz ($1/2$ pt)
$1 1/2$ cups	350 ml	12 fl oz
2 cups (1 pint)	500 ml	16 fl oz
$2 1/2$ cups	625 ml	20 fl oz (1 pint)
1 quart	1 liter	32 fl oz

Oven Temperature Equivalents

OVEN MARK	F	C	GAS
Very cool	250–275	130–140	$1/2$–1
Cool	300	150	2
Warm	325	170	3
Moderate	350	180	4
Moderately hot	375/400	190/200	5/6
Hot	425/450	220/230	7/8
Very hot	475	250	9